TABLE OF CONTENTS

TABLE OF CONTENTS.............................................................................................. i

ACRONYMS............................................................................................................. iii

ILLUSTRATIONS .................................................................................................... iv

TABLES ....................................................................................................................

CHAPTER 1 INTRODUCTION .................................................................................1

  Background ........................................................................................................... 2
  Primary Research Question ................................................................................. 6
    Secondary Research Questions .......................................................................... 6
  Significance ......................................................................................................... 6
  Assumptions......................................................................................................... 7
  Definitions ........................................................................................................... 7
  Limitations .......................................................................................................... 8
  Delimitations....................................................................................................... 8

CHAPTER 2 LITERATURE REVIEW ....................................................................11

  Framing Corruption .......................................................................................... 11
  Corruption in Context ....................................................................................... 14
  Utility of Corruption ......................................................................................... 19
  Empirical Studies.............................................................................................. 24
  Controlling Corruption ..................................................................................... 29
  Afghan Perceptions and Government Reports................................................... 33

CHAPTER 3 RESEARCH DESIGN .........................................................................40

Chapter 4 ANALYSIS ..............................................................................................46

  How do Afghans perceive corruption? .............................................................. 47
  How is bribery affecting Afghanistan's economic development?....................... 52
  What are U.S. perceptions of the Afghan culture of corruption? ..................... 64
  Is U.S. funding affecting corruption and economic development in Afghanistan?...... 69

CHAPTER 5 CONCLUSIONS AND RECOMMENDATIONS .......................................75

    Findings ........................................................................................................ 75
    Recommendations.......................................................................................... 77
        Diplomacy.............................................................................................. 77
        Information ............................................................................................ 80
        Military ................................................................................................. 82
        Economic .............................................................................................. 83
    Recommendations for Future Study .............................................................. 85
    Conclusion ................................................................................................... 86

GLOSSARY .............................................................................................................89

APPENDIX A CONSENT AND USE AGREEMENT FOR ORAL HISTORY
MATERIALS.............................................................................................................90

BIBLIOGRAPHY......................................................................................................91

# ACRONYMS

CPI          Corruption Perceptions Index

GDP        Gross Domestic Product

# ILLUSTRATIONS

Page

Figure 1. Causes of Corruption .................................................................................47

Figure 2. Corruption among Government Officials ...................................................50

Figure 3. Afghan Perception of Government Development ......................................51

Figure 4. Intermediaries in Bribery ..........................................................................55

Figure 5. Certainty of Bribes to get Government Service ........................................58

Figure 6. Non-State Justice Providers ......................................................................60

# TABLES

Page

Table 1.  Source and Variable Factors ................................................................44

Table 2.  Annual Economic Changes and U.S. Funding ......................................53

# CHAPTER 1

## INTRODUCTION

This study examines the costs and benefits of corruption with a focus on bribery in Afghanistan. The U.S. has been fighting an insurgency and trying to stabilize Afghanistan for the last ten years. The U.S. has spent $336 billion on security and stability operations in Afghanistan.[1] The Afghan leadership is resisting U.S. efforts to reduce corruption and becoming openly hostile toward further attempts to do so.[2] The U.S. government is frustrated with this resistance while it tries to establish stability by eliminating corruption.[3] Fiscal responsibility is of the utmost importance to the American public and costs need mitigation by leaders.[4] As the U.S. government looks to reduce poor spending habits, it must take a critical look at the funding for Afghanistan. Are Afghans so culturally bound to certain activities that they will not change? Is the Western perception of corruption through bribery hindering stability operations and economic development in Afghanistan? Is the U.S. government wasting funds trying to build a stable, self-sustained and secure Afghanistan? To answer these questions, this study will attempt to remove the moral considerations as well as the Westernized legal perceptions and look at the practices from a more utilitarian perspective. Is it viable to consider some instances where bribery, nepotism, and misappropriation can help create needed change in a society? This will help shape the timing of effective anti-corruption policy.

This chapter introduces the problem of corruption in Afghanistan and discusses some of the complexities of corruption that include legal, moral and cultural perspectives. Also included are a list of the primary and secondary research questions, assumptions, key definitions, limitations and delimitations. This chapter will conclude with a summary of the thesis' significance.

## Background

There are several definitions for corruption in literature. These definitions have changed over time and have branched apart from each other. The definition starts the initial confusion and contentions between what is corruption and what is not. Joseph Nye defines corruption as the behavior, which deviates from the formal duties of a public role because of private considerations (personal, family, and clique) or violates rules against the exercise of certain types of private-regarding influence.[5] Functionalists are theorists that view corruption as a positive means for achieving cultural development. Shahid Alam's examination on the functionalist's theories on corruption uses the following definition. Corruption is the sacrifice of the principal's interest for the agent's, or the violation of norms defining the agent's behavior.[6] Carl Friedrich formulates his definition based on Aristotle writings as "deviant behavior associated with a particular motivation, namely that of private gain at public expense."[7] The most common definition used in literature addressing economic impacts of corruption is the abuse of public office for private gain.[8]

Corruption has a moral, legal, and social standpoint. The moral and ethical dilemmas form the basis of frustrations and consternations amongst all people across societies. Gardner identifies moral and legal scenarios where a legal or moral argument for corruption can be unhinged using an example of a Nazi German passport inspector who accepts a bribe from a Jewish traveler trying to escape the country.[9] From a moral perspective this action would be justified, however at the time, the law forbade Jewish

2

emigration. In this case, an illegal action was moral in most regards. The bribe created the breach for the moral act to occur, which likely would not have been the case. Arguably, to reach this end without the bribe would be even more moral. The bribe acted as the tipping mechanism for globally moral action that was illegal in the country. This situation focuses on the act of bribery. Bribery is most common activity that is associated with corruption.

Gardner further cites the legal acts of U.S. Congress from the 1950s and 1960s that created an urban renewal program, clearing housing areas from several poor families in order to develop luxury living conditions and economic stimulating conditions.[10] In this historic scenario, several poor civilians became homeless and driven from their dilapidated conditions. The legal act executed and condoned would now face resistance from an immoral and entitlement perspective. This situation conflicts with the same moral grounds that made the illegal act in Germany acceptable. The conundrum that this creates is that the good of the majority outweighed the good of the minority. This minority were the poor and largely without a voice in the government. Although not necessarily corrupt, this scenario does bring to light the problem with separating pure moral and pure legal conditions for defining corruption. It also provides historical perspective of what was developmentally beneficial at the time against what is acceptable now.

These cases demonstrate problems with a pure legal perspective when considering what is legally corrupt or what is morally corrupt. Another perspective is to consider what is good for the public. The examination should be from what is good for the people and what aligns with what the people want. Determining the best actions to take for the country and balancing needs and wants are a culture's leaders concern and government's responsibility.

Referring back to Gardner scenario, the public opinion of Germany allowed the poor treatment of the Jews, regardless of the world's condemnation of this action as immoral [11] In the American case, there is an argument for the greater good of the public interest and economic development.[12] After considering these cases, a strictly moral perspective is not an appropriate lens to look at corruption as well. Moral views and laws governing actions vary largely from culture to culture. The viewpoint this research will take is one from an economic standpoint. The desired endpoint for operations in Afghanistan is one of providing stability. Stability is achieved though economic development and government legitimacy.

Corrupt acts are associated with the gain by the individual at the cost to the public. The initial focus is financial benefits gained through bribery, but corruption is not limited to monetary gains. Additional gains could be political or social power received from other acts associated with corruption. Corruption undermines a government's ability to develop and therefore support itself. One can broadly categorize corruption into cost-reducing, cost-enhancing, benefit-enhancing, and benefit-reducing activities.[13] Actions associated with corruption, such as bribery, patronage and nepotism, and misappropriations are common in developing countries.[14] This association creates the lack of bureaucratic institutions to mitigate it as well as the government's ability to affect it.

The identified practices associated with corruption are common practices in Iraq and Afghanistan and the U.S. military watch as criminals are released after capture without prosecution, contracted projects are inefficiently managed, and civic and command responsibilities are disregarded.[15] Americans are outraged and disgusted with the amount of "backdoor" activity encountered.[16] The host nation security forces, leaders, and communities just accept these practices as the norm. The experience in Iraq was the first real exposure by conventional U.S. forces to corruption practices in a Middle Eastern culture.[17] The lessons from the experience in Iraq are similar to experiences in developing Afghanistan's stability. Gardner notes, "There are nations where official corruption has been widespread for several years with no visible signs of outrage."[18] Afghanistan is one of the most corrupt countries in the world.[19] Although corruption is wholly condemned in the moral sense, there must be a consideration of potential benefit if it is culturally accepted.

A cultural perspective of corruption includes evaluating behavior such as bribery, nepotism, patronage, and misappropriation in regards to the country's norms. Afghan practices need scrutinized and compared to the cultural conditions associated with facilitating corruption. The theories suggesting corruption benefits economic development need considered and compared to the conditions in Afghanistan. By applying appropriate empirical models will determine the impact of corruption on Afghanistan's economy. These theories and models will determine if the U.S. actions in Afghanistan are appropriate and if the money provided in foreign aid and in support of stability operations is having the desired effect.

The hypotheses for each of the secondary questions below are:

1. Afghans perceive corruption as a normal means of doing business, and that the country has no reason to conform to Western bureaucratic practices.

5

2. Bribery is the means used as an unofficial tax collection to establish the government wealth and to supplement salaries of government employees by the users of the service provided.

3. The U.S. perceives Afghanistan as a corrupt society and the practices of nepotism and bribery are part of the culture.

4. Funding has a small positive effect on the economic development, whose minimal effects are due to accepting losses from bribery.

## Primary Research Question

How has U.S. funding in Stability Operations affected Corruption and Economic Development in Afghanistan?

## Secondary Research Questions

1. How do Afghans perceive corruption?

2. In the context of corruption, how is bribery affecting Afghanistan's Economic Development?

3. What are U.S. perceptions of the Afghan culture of corruption?

4. Is U.S. funding affecting corruption and economic development in Afghanistan?

## Significance

The purpose of this research is to determine how corruption is currently affecting the development of Afghanistan. The intent is to understand the development of corruption as practiced in Afghanistan and approach it from a neutral perspective to determine the impacts of corruption on economic development. This study will assess the effects of United States spending on contracts in support of stability operations as affected by the level of corruption and could be of significance to future legal, contracting, and logistic operations. The desired conclusion is to provide recommendations to shape the United State's efforts in effectively reducing corruption that both beneficial and receptive by the Afghan culture.

## Assumptions

This thesis assumes that the United States will continue to engage in global efforts to reduce the impacts of corruption, particularly in underdeveloped and transitioning economies. It also assumes that corrupt practices are not efficient, but do serve as a benefit for underdeveloped countries. The potential benefits serve as corrective actions for ineffective government policies and weak bureaucratic institutions needed for running a state and establishing a basis of trust among untrusting and tribal societies.

## Definitions

Bribery: Bribery is the act of offering or receiving a financial payment that is to dishonestly persuade (someone) to act in one's favor by a gift of money or other inducement.[20]

Misappropriation: Misappropriation is the illegal utilization or squandering of public resources for private-regarding uses.[21]

Nepotism: Nepotism is the practice among those with power or influence favoring relatives or friends, especially by providing jobs.[22]

Patronage: Patronage is the act of removing opposition political party office holders from political office after winning an election and granting these posts to their favorites.[23]

## Limitations

The primary limitation is the hidden and often illegal nature of corruption. There has been very little quantifiable data for researchers to measure the volume of corruption. As a result, the Corruption Perceptions Index (CPI) is a common measure for the level of corrupt activity within the country. The act of bribery is the most common activity associated with corruption and is the primary activity with a measurable economic cost to Afghanistan. This study will not identify a numerical cost to acts such as misappropriation or nepotism. The corruption perception index (CPI) includes these activities and are therefore justified in assessing the effects of corruption from a theoretical standpoint. The assessment of the circumstances in Afghanistan will determine which theorists and economic studies best match the effects of corruption to the economy.

## Delimitations

There will be no classified documents researched or referenced. This document will remain unclassified. Reviewed empirical studies will be limited to the last fifty years. The most recent valid studies will have higher emphasis. This study will only look at the quantified economic information from 2005 to 2010 to determine the appropriate theorist studies. It further will not examine the impacts and formations of criminal organizations that form although these organizations benefit from a corrupt environment. This study will also not evaluate U.S. or multinational anti-corruption initiatives outside of

Afghanistan.

---

[1]Amy Belasco, *The Cost of Iraq, Afghanistan, and Other Global Was on Terror Operation Since 9/*11 (Washington, DC: Congressional Research Service, 2010), http://www.au.af.mil/au/awc/awcgate/crs/rl33110.pdf (accessed 15 March 2011), 3

[2]Rajiv Chanrasekaren, "Karzai Rift Prompts U.S. to Reevaluate Anti-Corruption Strategy in Afghanistan," *The Washington Post*, April 2004, http://www.washington post.com/wp-dyn/content/article/2010/09/12/AR2010091203883.html (accessed 15 March 2011).

[3]Afghan Journalism Center, "Obama's Visit and Afghanistan's Corruption," http://www.ajc.af/english/component/content/article/47-category-name/84-obamas-visit-and-afghanistans-corruption (accessed 15 March 2011); WorldPublicOpinion.Org, "Afghan Approval of the Karzai Government and Western Forces, Though Still Strong, Is Declining," 14 December 2006, http://www.worldpublicopinion.org/pipa/articles/ brasiapacificra/290.php?nid=&id=&pnt=290&lb=bras (accessed 15 March 2011); Brigadier General H. R. McMaster (VTC Briefing to Training Centers of Influence, November 2010).

[4]U.S. Department of Defense, *Quadrennial Defense Review Report* (Washington, DC: Government Printing Office, February 2010), 75-80.

[5]Joseph S. Nye, "Corruption and Political Development: A Cost-Benefit Analysis," *The American Political Science Review* 61, no. 2 (1967): 419.

[6]Shahid Alam, "Anatomy of Corruption: An Approach to the Political Economy of Underdevelopment," *American Journal of Economics and Sociology* 48, no. 4 (October 1989): 442.

[7]Carl J. Friedrich, "Corruption Concepts in Historical Perspective," in *Political Corruption: Concepts and Contexts*, ed. Arnold Heidenheimer and Michael Johnson (New Brunswick, NJ: Transaction Publishers, 2002), 15.

[8]Daniel Treisman, "The Causes of Corruption: A Cross-National Study," *Journal of Public Economics* 76, no. 3 (June 2000): 399-457.

[9]John A. Gardiner, "Defining Corruption," in *Political Corruption: Concepts and Contexts*, ed. Arnold Heidenheimer and Michael Johnson (New Brunswick, NJ: Transaction Publishers, 2002), 30.

[10]Ibid., 31.

[11]Ibid., 30.

[12]Ibid., 31.

[13]Alam, 442-443.

[14]Nye, 419.

[15]Author's personal experience as a Military Transition Team Chief, Iraq (2009-2010).

[16]Chandraskaran; Gregory Douquet and Michael O'Hanlon, "A Realistic Anticorruption Strategy for Afghanistan," *The National Interest,* 13 October 2010, http://nationalinterest.org/commentary/realistic-anticorruption-4219 (accessed 15 March 2011); Author's personal assessment from personal reaction, conversations with other Soldiers while deployed and Soldiers upon return that had similar experiences.

[17]Wayne Sandholtz and William Koetzle, "Accounting for Corruption: Economic Structure, Democracy, and Trade," *International Studies Quarterly* 44 (2000): 35.

[18]Gardiner, 38.

[19]Transparency International, "Corruption Perceptions Index, 2010," http://www.transparency.org/policy_research/surveys_indices/cpi/2010/results (accessed 15 March 2011).

[20]Oxford Dictionary, s.v. "bribery," http://oxforddictionaries.com (accessed 15 March 2011).

[21]Nye, 419.

[22]Oxford Dictionary, s.v. "nepotism," http://oxforddictionaries.com (accessed 15 March 2011).

[23]Gardiner, 27.

CHAPTER 2

LITERATURE REVIEW

This study examines the costs and benefits of the westernized view of corruption. The ideas that inform this research are from books authored by noted professionals in political science, sociology and economics who have studied corruption. It will rely on scholarly articles published in professional journals and research papers. The author will reference government reports and recent news articles for current events in regards to corruption.

The purpose is to evaluate existing literature relevant to the thesis and identify similarities and gaps. The chapter will address literature in five distinct areas: (1) political theories of corruption, (2) empirical measures of the impacts on development, (3) controlling corruption, (4) Afghan governmental trends and perceptions of corruption, and (5) Afghan culture.

The following chapter discusses the literature used to answer the research questions. Each work will present the general topic and specific subject. It will then present the purpose of each article and describe the methodology. Each article will end with an assessment of its application to the research questions.

Framing Corruption

Corruption is a difficult practice to truly define or understand. Generally, corruption has negative connotations. Corruption has aspects in the moral, legal, ethical, political, economic, and cultural arenas. Arnold Heidenheimer brings several of the professional articles together in his political corruption collection.[1] Corruption is most

11

recently the focus of studies and debates. Heidenheimer's collection provides insight into corruption by presenting qualitative contrasts across several countries from the currently successful to those economically failing. The literature also provides contributions from authors that analyze corruption across several disciplines extending from history, sociology, political science, economics, and anthropology. As the global economy grows, it is becoming more and more of a concern because of the potential impacts on the world as a whole.

Carl Friedrich provides a historical perspective of corruption as it changes over time. He references philosophers such as Plato, Aristotle and Machiavelli.[2] Plato introduces the initial analyses of corruption as human flaw introduced into governments that distorts and perverts them. Aristotle takes Plato further by identifying the transformation of a monarchy into a tyrant, aristocracy into an oligarchy, and a democracy into mob rule. Aristotle identifies the leadership of a corrupt government as shifting from the general or public interest to personal interest. Machiavelli introduces corruption as the process of degradation of the virtue of the citizen.[3] This begins the shift of the person being the source of corruption to the institution causing the corruption of the person.

The fore mentioned philosophers describe man's greed as the source of corruption and allude to corrupt rulers serving themselves and not the people. This article highlights the longevity of corruption and attempts to isolate the purest of terms for it. From these perspectives, it makes it difficult to identify a single act as corrupt or not, but the intention for which it was conducted, regardless of law. To address corruption Rousseau adapted Machiavelli's perspective with an examination of corruption by examining

Sparta's defense to corruption. Rousseau championed that public opinion could be the best defense and that the political system corrupts the man.[4] This introduced that flaws in the system allowed for morality to become corrupt. In this changed views from humans being a naturally corrupt to weak institutions corrupting the man. Regardless of the source of the corruption, Rousseau identified that strengthening institutions would weaken the opportunity for corruption to flourish.

John Gardiner explores the difficulty in defining corruption.[5] Gardner's examination considered the differences in laws of various nations, the considerations of the public's opinion and the effects on the public. Each of these different perspectives provides different challenges for defining corruption.

Legal definitions are convenient because they contain clear requirements within statutes that codify conditions and justify punishment for violators. However, they are subjective to the regimes that are in power. An oppressive regime for example may not call activities it engages in as corrupt. These further have the assumption that what is legal is also ethical, which is a problem with moralist opinions of corruption. Laws further become separating line with the differences in norms and laws between nations. Impacts of legal systems are also subject to comparison complications when comparing better systems between a country with a large public sector and a small one. Legal systems create a further dilemma if illegal actions are unenforceable.

The enforcement of law is largely a factor by public opinion. Public opinion causes varying definitions between legal definitions of corruption among cultures. There are a couple of problems that result from this perspective of definitions, these are the difficulty in enforcing a law that is largely against public opinion, identifying who is considered the "public" (voters, adults, males), and that opinion changes over time.[6] These complications contribute to Heidenheimer's assessment that of the differences between white, grey and black corruption discussed later in this thesis.

The final consideration for defining corruption in Gardner's study lies in public interest. Public interest focuses on the affect a particular act has on the majority of the public as opposed to the acts legality or morality. This definition is complicated because of confusion and discrimination of who are the public. These variations create the moralistic, traditionalistic or individualistic tendencies of different cultures.

Heidenheimer warns of growing corruption and categorizes acts associated with corruption as white, grey and black corruption.[7] White corruption is the small and petty activities that are easily accepted and normal activities. Gray corruption is the nebulous area expanding from not liked, but tolerated and accepted because nothing can be done about it activities. Black corruption is wholly wrong and not accepted by public norms. The process of graying is the steady growth of gray activities turning white and the list of black activities entering the grey area. The increasing of acceptable actions fosters the problems countries face with a history of corruption.

## Corruption in Context

The following section begins by looking at actions that are corrupt by modern western standard. It will then examine works from authors who analyzed the impacts of corruption and its causes from other countries perspectives and from other times. This will help break the purely western and mature society's perspective and prejudice.

Koenraad Sward examined the sale of government office as it was in Europe and other countries in the 17th century.[8] His study takes a historical look at politically and

14

economically why these practices were necessary and appropriate at the time. Dependent upon the country, these government positions sold could be temporary or permanently treated as property that could be further sold or inherited. The arguments in favor of the sale of offices included the reduction of bureaucracy and increase to the government's funds. This method, with the class systems of the time, also allowed access to government by the middle class and elimination of favoritism. Sward identifies that as societies developed, the reasons and support for the sale of office no longer existed.[9] This assessment needs considered for all practices considered corrupt by current western standards. Doing so will help identify practices that may have utility and are culturally acceptable, and it will focus efforts in eliminating truly harmful practices.

Vito Tanzi provides one of the few studies of the impacts of nepotism on a countries development.[10] Tanzi begins highlighting the Chinese word of "guanxi," which means connections. These connections are similar to the practices of nepotism and patronage in Afghanistan. He discusses several scenarios where the use of connections influenced decisions on policy makers or people of power. Tanzi offers the "arm's length principle" which states that personal relationships should place no role in economic decisions that involve more than one person.[11] Deviation from this principle violates otherwise equal opportunities and fair competition. Tanzi references an article in *The Economist* in 1992 by Prakash Reddy.[12] This article described a social anthropologist from India's experiences of two city's social dynamic. One was a city in Denmark, where social interaction with family and neighbors were limited. This was associated to ideal conditions for economic theories. The other city was one in India, where families interacted daily and relationships outweighed normal economic decisions. In the Indian scenario, the civil servants would have a propensity to deviate from the arm's length principle and in fact, if they would not show preference to family, they would be social outcasts. Tanzi states that developing countries prefer the Indian model to the village in Denmark.[13]

Fair competition is a principle in economic theory that state if markets were perfect, then government would not need to play a role. Because markets are not fair, the state in practice must engage in acts of taxation, public spending, transfers, lending, etc. In an ideal government, people act in the best interest of the public welfare and are otherwise neutral and impartial. Because ideal conditions are often not the case, Tanzi refers to Coleman who criticizes economic theory and introduces the concept of social capital.[14]

Social capital deals with direct and indirect influences in the perfect competition theory. Coleman's criticism is "the fiction that society consists of a set of independent individuals, each of whom acts to achieve goals that are independently arrived at, and that the functioning of the social system consists of the combination of their actions of independent individuals."[15] Coleman's arguments are that people are not wholly selfish, people do not operate alone, nor are their goals independently driven. The "social capital" is the collection of favors and social contacts that an individual has.

"Social capital" supports corrupt networks, in particular the networks that practice nepotism or bribery. Shared risk in the conduct of illicit acts builds trust relationships. The relationships affect the arbitrary execution of rules, regulations, execution of permits and credit. It also provides conditions for unfair advantages in competition from outside entrepreneurs who develop local monopolies and thus limit efficiencies derived from competition. Nepotism also affects the fair and efficient hiring and promotion of individuals based on competency, which can also hurt development and incentives for education and pursuing needed skills.[16] However, this process does grant implicit trust because of personal connections.

Voskanyan studied the effects of corruption on the development of Armenia.[17] The practices of corruption are similar in regards to identifying bribery, nepotism, and misappropriation. Voskanyan identifies a weak appreciation for the rule of law and lack of accountability of public officials as the reason for corruption.[18] He introduces a psychological argument that perpetrates corruption, arguing that fear of not conforming to "the publically perceived way of life" keeps people from changing their norms. Voskanyan associates this fear with Armenia being a formerly communist country. Voskanyan refers to Leslie Holmes' "the power of both peer-pressure and peer-comparison can be great, for instance in the words of one artist: when the best of people take bribes, isn't it the fool who doesn't?"[19] Voskanyan also refers to Jim Saxton when discussing the impact foreign aid has on a countries development.[20] He asserts that foreign government aid increases corruption by promoting the strength of the government sector relative to the private sector. This perspective may have significance due to the previous Soviet activity in Afghanistan and similarities between cultures.

Aaron Tornell discusses capital flight, which is the most critical outcome of corruption.[21] Capital flight emerges when one attempts to place his wealth beyond the reach of competing groups. Jess Benhabib discusses the social games that occur amongst those with consolidated wealth, carries this concept further.[22] These public elites play a game that translates to strategic behaviors that result in overconsumption, and diversion

17

of resources to safeguard them from appropriation from other players. These capital games involve the elusive actions of corruption amongst the social and governmental elites. These actions are either legal or not identified as illegal. They help country elites maintain a financial advantage over foreign competitors. This capital flight is why development rarely occurs in countries with high corruption.

Myint-U provides a review of some of the basic concepts of corruption.[23] Myint-U indicates corruption exists in both developed and developing nations and in public and private sectors to include non-profit organizations. He summarizes the negative impacts most empirical studies determine between corruption and development, and further provides an extensive list of various corrupt behaviors. Myint-U associates the causes of corruption by weakness of government institutions, little oversight into activities, and high levels of discretionary power on the part of the individual or business. His conclusion is to combat corruption by undertaking political and economic reform to reduce institutional weaknesses. This document reinforces common themes regarding relationships between corruption and bureaucracy as well as providing a basic direction for reducing corruption.

Attempting to understand corruption involves looking at it from more than a single, biased view. Corruption is not a new topic for theory, and has continuously exists in all societies. The level of corruption grows and shrinks over time. From a western, developed nation's perception, corruption is morally wrong, economically inefficient, and legally wrong. It is difficult to separate the moral and ethical connections to corruption, but theories indicate that utility may exist. This utility of corruption needs examined for merit. This potential merit comes from the existence of historical examples of corrupt

activities that led to economic development and moral changes in a country.

## Utility of Corruption

This section will draw out the political theories of corruption. Several theorists

identify potential benefits for the practices that western and modernized societies call

corrupt. In modern societies, many of the proposed utilities no longer apply as a benefit.

Some of the practices align with cultural challenges and practices or facilitate

developmental learning through the transition into modernization. In western haste to

assist non-modern countries accelerate through development, they overlook the

importance of these hard-learned lessons.

Nathaniel Leff challenges the moralizing rationale.[24] He examines scenarios

where bureaucracy and cultures limit development and identifies where corrupt activities

help breach the political obstacles. Leff contests that corruption has positive effects for

increasing economic activities with a government that is either hostile or indifferent to

entrepreneurs.[25] He states that bribes increase an entrepreneur's ability to quickly enter a

market or introduce innovative ideas without the need to establish personal relationships.

Leff also states that bribery to receive contracts support competition in the manner that

only the most efficient contractor will offer the highest amount to the government agent

and still be profitable.[26] Leff justifies the bribe as a means for getting political advocacy

for agents that normally would not have a voice in government and help bridge natural

trust gaps that exist in a culture. He concludes that policy may be the problem and not

corruption.[27] This provides a justification for individual or group action that is either

illegal or "corrupt" to serve as developmental solution for a corrupt or weak government.

19

Leff is often cited for his theories on the utility of corruption and highlights several

considerations for corruption to be beneficial in social, political, and economic terms.

Samuel P. Huntington discusses how corruption exists in all societies and that it

becomes more common at particular times in a societies evolution.[28] He discusses

practices of developing, pre-modern societies. These societies accept patronage,

favoritism, and the appropriation of public funds for personal use as acceptable or

legitimate forms of behavior. Huntington's view is that this persists through the

modernization process.[29] Modernization enhances corruption due to confusion over the

issue of what is in the public and what is the private domain. As a society transitions, the

new rules needed for expanding the state in economic and social spheres lead to increased

bureaucratic controls. The increase of these controls cut into profitability of businesses

and entice corruption. In order to stop this string of corruption, the state attempts to

impose further bureaucratic measures. This develops conditions where corruption is

necessary for any progress. Huntington also identifies that as people come across new

wealth they will use this wealth to secure power. This further addresses the introduction

of foreign players to the society who has no interest in conforming the social values and

norms. Huntington provides developmental considerations for why corruption is a

commonality among developing nations and why corruption often is a precursor to

development.[30] His assessment for effective reduction efforts require a scaling of the

norms associated with the behavior of public officials, ultimately a slow transition

between the norms that exist in a pre-modern society to legalized practices that are

acceptable in a modernized society.

Joseph Nye provides a balanced approach to reasons why corruption has developed in cultures.[31] His study separates the moralist or revisionist perspectives. He acknowledges times in U.S. and British history where corruption helped development. Nye assumes that legitimacy and effectiveness link in the "long run," but can compensate for each other in the "short run."[32] Nye's examination further explores Leff's theories on the potential benefits of corruption, which could lead to economic development, national integrations, and increased government capacity of new states. Nye compares this to probabilities of waste in resources, investment distortions, instability, and loss of legitimacy. Nye produces a scoring matrix to attempt to refine the general statements and theories of corruption and development. Nye ultimately concludes that, except for "top level corruption," that it is probable that the cost of corruption is less in developing countries.[33] Nye's study indicates that corruption can be of benefit if it is the only solution to obstacles for development.

Susan Rose-Ackerman examines the theoretical arguments by revisionists.[34] She looks at bribery as harmful in nearly all cases by looking at it from a realist's perspective. Rose-Ackerman argues that public officials may initially be motivated to perform better by receiving speed or incentive monies; however, this practice will result in no work performed unless there is a bribe.[35] The destructive nature of bribes will encourage officials to create false scarcities in order to encourage bribes for their time or assistance. Rose-Ackerman challenges the validity of Leff's argument by stating that the most efficient contractor will not be the one to pay the highest bribe, the true costs will end up being in unproductive cuts in material or transferred costs to the population.[36] She states that the most harmful form of corruption is in the form of capital flight.[37] Because of corruptions nature and lack of records of bribes, there is nothing prohibiting money from leaving the country or tracking the actual costs. This ultimately is the most damaging effect of corruption.

Simcha Werner examines Israeli history in order to examine the claims of the functional dysfunction of corruption.[38] The functional claims are that it bypasses cumbersome economic and legal regulations, foster integration, institutionalize party building, and serve as an advocate to rigid or uncaring authorities. He challenges the theory that corruption naturally expires when it has served its purpose and instead proposes that corruption has a lifecycle where it matures and shifts to current conditions.[39] Werner's examination began with the pre-state conditions of Palestine. The Turkish style of government was heavy with nepotism, extortion, and bribery, which maintained a cultural divide between the Arab upper class and the Jewish peasants and working class. In this system, the Arabs maintained the ability to create personal profit through political and proprietary rights. The Jewish people had several factions and backgrounds and the semblance of political parties, which relied on patron-client relationships. The Jewish collective sustainment came from philanthropy.[40]

This government structure was subject to a quick change when Britain received responsibility for Palestine in 1922. The British introduced western styles of government that included a bureaucratic system of merit oriented administration, laws, and regulations. Because the Jewish system of self-government better matched the western form of government, they received more responsibility and eventual dominance over the newly forming Israel. The Arabs seemed to cripple the development of the nation with their corrupt practices. Jewish behaviors set the conditions for government institutions to modernize and develop into profitable growth. However, political and cultural norms adjusted to the economic changes when more Jews began to return to Israel. Similar corrupt practices of the Arabic led period began to resurface and practices that were illegal during British leadership slowly began to erode and become acceptable practice.[41] Werner references Heidenheimer's "graying" corruption as Israel continued along history and accepted more corrupt activity as routine activities. Werner introduced the concept that corruption has a level of equilibrium. He proposes that corruption wanes and returns as it adjusts to changing bureaucracies. This proposal emphasizes the connotation that corruption is politically pandemic, just as a virus is in human biology. After Werner's study of Israel, he determines that corruption is not necessarily a product of modernization. He assesses that it will not die away in transition as it pushes past bureaucratic or development hurtles. Werner reemphasizes that while corrupt practices are condoned and rationalized, more damaging forms of corruption will become acceptable.[42]

Corruption can co-exist with economic development. An anonymous author, identified as Candidate 40801, explores the success that South East Asia had experiences from the 1960s through the 1990s despite having high levels of corruption.[43] The growth and corruption levels seem to run contrary to the common understanding of corruption being completely harmful. Candidate 40801 identifies that despite the existence of weak businesses and informal markets that a strong state government can force the co-existence with corruption and economic growth.[44] This co-existence is explained by Pei "emphasis on growth in East Asia has a political origin: authoritarian regimes ruled in all high-performance East Asian economies . . . maintaining high growth rates was and is regarded as essential for building not just industrial economies, but the political legitimacy or ruling elites."[45]

Candidate 40801 references Xu who stated that the close relation between state and business facilitated the growth by granting special privileges and interest rates to each other.[46] This facilitated the illusion of growth through recycling funds throughout the government despite some poor investments. The fact that capital was staying within the country was what truly supported the growth during this period. However, despite monies remaining within borders, places like the Philippines still lost more money than what they owe in their national debt.[47]

The government inefficiency bridges into the intangible cost of corruption. Candidate 40801 summarizes an African study, which lists the immeasurable costs of corruption.[48] This study concluded that corruption intensified ethnic conflict, ruined efficiency of government, crippled the merit system of hiring and promotion, and generated an atmosphere of distrust throughout administration. Before the conclusion, one final note of risk was associated with the Asian financial crisis. The crony capitalism system used to develop growth through the relationships inevitably failed due to large sums of capital invested in poorly vetted programs.[49] In addition, the failures of one corrupt participant created a ripple effect through the whole system. These insights to corruption provide a potential best-case scenario for Afghanistan.

## Empirical Studies

The Transparency International's corruption perception index (CPI) measures perceived corruption levels of a country. This index is the product of ten separate surveys that sample business professionals, consultant, government, and local populations.

24

International organizations develop separate surveys that measure political, economic and managerial risks and improper practices that are constantly reviewed and updated.[50] The combined results create the perceived corruption score. A country with a high-perceived level of corruption will have a low score on the index.

Transparency International's index shows western countries as having low corruption. Western standards potentially biased the surveys used to identify corrupt activities. The countries with higher scores (less corrupt) tend to have the higher Gross Domestic Product (GDP).[51] Does this mean that western practices and definitions of corruption are more complete or better, or does this mean that with current levels of development in terms of GDP have they exhausted the utility of corruption? Many of the empirical researchers use the corruption perception index (CPI) to establish relationships with various economic, political, and cultural components in a country's development.[52]

Paolo Mauro examines relationships between corruption and investment, bureaucratic efficiency, and political stability.[53] Through an empirical study, he develops linkages with corruption and instability and finds them intrinsically related. Mauro notes that countries that are politically unstable spend less on education and have less foreign and domestic investment.[54] Instability, investment, and education are all factors of economic development. This study also identifies a positive correlation between bureaucratic efficiency and political stability. Based on this the logical conclusion is that corrupt practices are related to bureaucratic inefficiencies.

Kwabena Gyimah-Brempong studies the effects of corruption on economic growth and wealth distribution.[55] He studies discusses the impacts of corruption in Africa. Africa has a similar corruption rating as Afghanistan and faces many of the same

25

cultural trends regarding acceptable corrupt practices and tribal pride. The empirical study determines that corruption decreases a countries growth rate as well as increases the inequality of wealth distribution. Gyimah-Brempong's study concludes that as countries sent more money from foreign aid into the country that it enlarges the inequality gap between the power brokers and people.[56] His suggestion is to promote development in these countries by helping to eliminate corruption instead of supplying funds to government.

Jani Saastamoinen (2006) examines the interdependence between wealth distribution and economic growth.[57] Unequal wealth distribution is a byproduct of corruption. Wealth enhances growth in terms of being able to save more and thus have a higher rate of accumulation as well as the capacity to absorb large sunk costs in investments. However, wealth investment in productive capital does not occur. The empirical study conducted indicated no statistical consensus on whether wealth distribution itself deters growth. Saastamoinen does conclude that wealth redistribution needs to occur to ensure stability and to enhance development in the form of encouraged labor force, education, and health programs.[58]

Daniel Treisman is a well-cited author who takes a cross-national approach to determining and understanding the causes of corruption.[59] His article assesses the corruption index across several countries with high corruption levels. Treisman theorizes on the cultural and historic aspects that result in corruption.[60] This includes cultural norms of accepting and offering bribes as a normal practice to a distrust of private agents. Treisman notes that public abuse is a consequence of the new sources of wealth and power influence available in a time when the regulatory authority in not yet established.

Treisman conducts an empirical study that compares the per capita gross national product, federal state structure, and British colonial backgrounds of fifty countries across Asia, Africa, Europe, Latin America, and the Middle East. Treisman's results shows statistical significance to inverse relations with democratic right and corruption.[61] This study shows that the stronger democratic systems have a lower level of corruption. Statistical results also showed that being a former British colony results in lower corruption.[62] The element of adding the historical ties to British colonies appears as a random factor, but countries with former British ties tend to have western style governance. Western institutions may be more effective in countering acts of corruption, but it also may provide a skewed perspective on what indicators determine the score on the corruption perceptions index. This document is the first reviewed that includes a transnational comparison with a cultural focus on the Middle East region. These theories apply to Afghanistan because of their mistrust of outsiders. There are also the similarities with the level of nepotism in the country. Treisman's association with British colonial relations supports the concept that the Transparency International Index may possess western perceptions.

Wayne Sandoltz examines the interrelations between corruption and economic levels of a country as well as its extent of state control, integration into the world economy and share of the population's Protestant religious affiliation.[63] The religious aspects are a continuation of Treisman's study resulting in significance to British colonial background to a lower perceived corruption level. Sandholtz's empirical study examines fifty countries to compare the perceived level of corruption against these factors to determine if corruption is predictable by the associated levels of development in these categories.[64]

Sandholtz argues that relatively low-income correlates to higher levels of corruption since incentives for supplemental monies are greater and hypothesizes that strong democratic institution and long-standing democracies will correlate negatively to corruption.[65] He states democratic institutions are dependent upon equality and openness to be successful. In order for these to become strong, the public must create the norms that hold corruption as antagonistic to basic values. Global integration also runs negatively to corruption. The argument for this is that the less the level of corruption the greater the confidence foreign investors have in the security and stability of the market and that there be a higher demand on transparency.

The statistical tests showed the appropriate correlation hypothesized. Lower levels of corruption is associated with higher average income, lower state controls over the economy, greater integration in the international economy, stronger democracy, and prevalence of Protestant religion. Outliers to the test included Italy and Belgium who's practices of patronage and political policies provided an unaccounted for deviation. In these countries, the elites have great ability to distribute goods to gain loyalty from the community.[66]

Ali Kutan does an empirical study that focuses on sixteen Middle Eastern countries and compares them to eighteen Latin American countries from 1993 to 2003.[67] This study examines two regions of relatively similar development and corruption levels.[68] It conducts a cross-cultural study on the effects of corruption on growth of per capita GDP and labor force. The results of the empirical testing demonstrated that the

Middle East did experience growth in per capita income despite corruption. Kutan associated this growth with the oil sector in the Middle East. He asserts that countries with a single natural resource as a source of wealth are likely to cut through bureaucratic red tape with corruption to facilitate business.[69]

Swaleheen conducts an empirical study that accounts for the joint relationships for economic growth, corruption and investment.[70] The study attempts to synchronize the effects that each have on a country and then applies an economic freedom variable to determine the effect of bureaucracy has on free trade.[71] Swaleheen uses an econometric model to account for growth measured in school enrollment rates, size of government, and political stability, and population growth. He then developed standards for measuring investment and corruption.[72] The model then utilizes a separate variable to account for the interaction between corrupting and economic freedom. This variable comes from the Economic Freedom Index. The results of Swaleheen's model find that corruption lowers growth when economic freedom is low, but economic freedoms in high corruption increases growth.[73] Swaleheen deduced that the results supported Leff's theory with the utility corruption in regards to providing an effective circumvention of excess bureaucratic policies.[74] This contradicts most models that determine corruption as wholly damaging to growth. He compares corruption as expansive and restrictive. Swaleheen's conclusion is that corruption may be helpful, but corruption needs reduced after it serves its purposed or else it becomes a political or bureaucratic impediment to development.[75]

## Controlling Corruption

Robert Klitgaard weaves in several working anti-corruption programs throughout his book to illustrate some of his key points.[76] The first of which is that corruption cannot be eliminated. Second, there is an optimal degree of corruption. The balance between the cost of fighting corruption and the cost of corruption to a country is the optimal level.[77] Klitgaard addresses the cost of combating corruption and states "the optimal level of corruption is not zero."[78] This combines Werner's observations of corruptions lifecycle of corruption with the economic law of diminishing returns.[79] Klitgaard acknowledge that on occasion, corruption may be efficient as Leff and Huntington indicated, but ultimately in a society where corruption in continuous, there is likely no improvement.[80]

Klitgaard discusses the base elements for measuring corruption-containing agents with monopoly power over clients, with great discretionary power and weak accountability to the principle. His equation of corruption is: Corruption equals Monopoly Power, plus Discretionary Power, minus Accountability.[81] Klitgaard discusses several options within categories to address the components of corruption. Options include selection of agents, adjusting reward and penalty policies, gathering of information from the public, restructuring the client-agent relationship, and ultimately changing the attitudes towards corruption.[82]

Throughout his book, he highlights stories of countries that had significant corruption problems. Each of these countries made positive steps to reducing the corruption level. These countries like those in South East Asia and Latin America have had developmental and cultural challenges to change both the empowered elite and the common acceptance to abhorrent behavior. Klitgaard closes his book with implementation of strategies that involve identifying not only the problem, but also appropriate fixes. The fixing strategy involves getting the political and public support for anti-corruption efforts before attempting to implement a change.[83] Without the commitment from the leadership or people to hold them accountable, any attempts of proposing a plan will simply result in lip service. Klitgaard also recommends finding a moral role model within the country as a leader to support the change of the corrupt behaviors.[84] Kitgaard concludes with a forewarning that the implementation of any plan will cause turbulence in the country.[85]

Daniel Kaufmann reviews many of the cases that Rose-Ackerman used to discredit the arguments in favor of corruption as posed by Leff.[86] He points out the evidence that corruption slows foreign direct investment.[87] Foreign direct investment is positively associated with a country's economic development. Kaufmann does acknowledge that underdeveloped or over cumbersome bureaucratic policies may resort to corrupt activities, but in large the benefits associated with corruption are illusionary.[88] Kaufmann provides a thorough framework and process for institutional reform.[89] The reforms involve finding honest leadership and incorporation of international agencies to help support and frame the changes. Institutional reform includes economic, government, and legal reforms. Kaufmann states the key to success is to maintain visibility and accountability on anti-corruption developments within the International community as well as holding public educational conferences.[90] In a survey held by Kaufmann in 1996, several elite members of corrupt countries acknowledged large domestic responsibility to the corruption levels in their counties, but two-thirds of them also contributed it to foreign corruption as a problem that also needs addressed.[91]

David Chaikin addresses a direct approach to holding governmental leaders accountable.[92] Chaikin indentifies the secrecy of banking institutions, such as Swiss bank accounts further capital corruption and capital flight.[93] Part of the difficulty in finding where the money moved to freezing and seizing the stolen assets and returning them to the government is the lack of institutional transparency. Chaikin suggests several legal changes to address the current challenges for this type of a program.[94] Chaikin asserts that the money appropriated through bribery is the countries taxes and is therefore property of the state.[95] He further connects this assertion to officials with access to government money or assets either simply stole or made financial gains through misappropriation.[96] Extradition laws need established to bring the person to justice in the event of flight. Strict international laws and transparency will reduce the likelihood of capital flight. The money stolen from the government from bribes, theft, and misappropriation needs put back into government hands and not subject to legal claims of third parties against the former elite. Chaikin identifies that the loss of government funds through capital flight perpetuates a continuing spiral of debt and poor accountability.[97] The legal process to confiscate funds from fleeing elites need to be speedily processed through the judiciary. To further assist openness of banking laws to facilitate tracking and accounting for these funds must occur.

Zoe Pearson builds on the international responsibility to solve corruption.[98] She recognizes the same components to reduce corruption as Rose-Ackerman, such as increase the likeliness of being caught, increase the punishments, and decrease the discretionary powers of the agents to reduce the incentives.[99] Pearson argues that if a regime does not adopt the institutional and administrative reforms and commit to them then the international community can and should intervene. The argument comes in the form of human rights based on the Limburg Principles or Maastrict Guidelines.[100]

## Afghan Perceptions and Government Reports

The Brookings Institution provides quantitative measures and indicators for the conditions in Afghanistan.[101] They provide measures for the Afghanistan's Security, Governance and Rule of Law, Economic and Quality of Life, and Public Opinion. This will provide measurable sources to determine the level of readiness the Afghan people are in accepting or implementing potential anti corruption practices.

Integrity Watch Afghanistan focuses on research, monitoring and advocacy on anti-corruption and pro-integrity work in Afghanistan through networks with sub-national and community based organizations in a variety of districts.[102] They performed a national survey in 2010 that measured many aspects of corruption and perceptions of the people. This provided measure percentages, frequencies, and locations of where corruption is heaviest in the eyes of the people.

The Report to Congressional Committees: Afghanistan from the U.S. Government Accountability Office reports key issues for congressional oversight.[103] The report covers developments in U.S. commitments, security, economic development, governance, and oversight of contractor performance as well as other issues. This document outlines the historical financial inputs into Afghanistan.

The U.S. Government Accountability Office also provides documentation and reports for recent assessments leading to change in activities and management in Afghanistan.[104] Contract management has recently become a great concern due to vulnerabilities for fraud. Organizations created in 2008 to correct deficiencies addressed were Army Contracting Command and Expeditionary Contracting Command. Additionally, a Special Inspector General to Afghanistan Reconstruction investigates all financial transactions in Afghanistan. These reports collect lessons learned as well as

provide a basis for consideration on U.S. activities effects since 2008.

[1] Arnold Heidenheimer and Michael Johnson, *Political Corruption: Concepts and Contexts* (New Brunswick, NJ: Transaction Publishers, 2002).

[2] Freidrich, 15-18.

[3] Ibid.

[4] Friedrich, 19.

[5] Gardiner, 25-39.

[6] Ibid.

[7] Arnold Heidenheimer, "Perspectives on the Perception of Corruption," in *Political Corruption: Concepts and Contexts*, ed. Arnold Heidenheimer and Michael Johnson (New Brunswick, NJ: Transaction Publishers, 2002), 141-154.

[8] Koenraad Sward, "The Sale of Public Offices," in *Political Corruption: Concepts and Contexts*, ed. Arnold Heidenheimer and Michael Johnson (New Brunswick, NJ: Transaction Publishers, 2002), 95-106.

[9] Sward, 102.

[10] Vito Tanzi, "Corruption: Arm's-length Relationships and Markets," in *The Economics of Organized Crime*, ed. Gianluca Fiorentini and Sam Peltzman (Cambridge, UK: Cambridge University Press 1995), 161-181.

[11] Tanzi, 163-164.

[12] Ibid., 164-165.

[13] Ibid.

[14] J. S. Coleman, "Foundations on Social Theory," in *The Economics of Organized Crime*, ed. Gianluca Fiorentini and Sam Peltzman (Cambridge, UK: Cambridge University Press 1995), 166.

[15] Ibid.

[16] Tanzi, 171.

[17]Frunzik Voskanyan, "A Study of the Effects of Corruption on Economic and Political Development in Armenia" (Masters thesis, American University of Armenia, 2000).

[18]Voskanyan, 18.

[19]Leslie Holmes, *The End of Communist Power* (New York: Oxford University Pressm 1993), 170.

[20]Voskanyan, 26.

[21]Aaron Tornell and Andres Velasco, "Why Does Capital Flow from Poor to Rich Countries? Interest Groups and Dynamic Games in Poor Countries," *Journal of Political Economy* 100 (August 2002): 1208-1231.

[22]Jess Benhabib and Aldo Rustichini, "Social Conflict, Growth and Income Distribution," *Journal of Economic Growth* 1 (1996): 125-142.

[23]Thant Myint-U, "Corruption: Causes, Consequences and Cures," *Asia-Pacific Development Journal* 7, no. 2 (December 2000): 33-58.

[24]Leff, 307.

[25]Ibid., 313.

[26]Ibid., 314.

[27]Ibid., 307-320.

[28]Samuel P. Huntington, "Modernization and Corruption," in *Political Corruption: Concepts and Contexts*, ed. Arnold Heidenheimer and Michael Johnson (New Brunswick, NJ: Transaction Publishers, 2002), 253.

[29]Huntington, 254.

[30]Ibid., 253-263.

[31]Nye, 417-427.

[32]Ibid., 418.

[33]Ibid., 427.

[34]Susan Rose-Ackerman, "When is Corruption Harmful," in *Political Corruption: Concepts and Contexts*, ed. Arnold Heidenheimer and Michael Johnson (New Brunswick, NJ: Transaction Publishers, 2002), 353-371.

[35]Rose-Ackerman, 357.

[36]Ibid., 358.

[37]Ibid., 364-365.

[38]Simcha B. Werner, "The Development of Political Corruption in Israel," in *Political Corruption: Concepts and Contexts*, ed. Arnold Heidenheimer and Michael Johnson (New Brunswick, NJ: Transaction Publishers, 2002), 199-220.

[39]Werner, 199.

[40]Ibid., 202.

[41]Ibid., 211.

[42]Ibid., 217.

[43]Candidate 40801, "What is the Impact of Corruption on Economic Development in the Newly Industrialized Countries of South East Asia?" Political Corruption, L2046, benaston.com/.../What%20is%20the%20impact%20of%20Corruption%20o... United Kingdom (URL incomplete: found on Googledocs accessed 15 March 2011), 15-25.

[44]Candidate 40801, 15.

[45]Pei.

[46]Tzong-Shian Yu and Dianqing Xu, eds. "From Crisis to Recovery: East Asia Rising Again?" in "What is the Impact of Corruption on Economic Development in the Newly Industrialized Countries of South East Asia?" Political Corruption, L2046, Candidate 40801, benaston.com/.../What%20is%20the%20impact%20of%20 Corruption%20o... United Kingdom (URL incomplete: found on Googledocs accessed 15 March 2011), 16.

[47]Candidate 40801, 18.

[48]Ibid., 19.

[49]Ibid., 23.

[50]Transparency International.

[51]U.S. Central Intelligence Agency, World Fact Book, "Country Comparison: GDP," https://www.cia.gov/library/publications/the-world-factbook/rankorder/ 2001rank.html (accessed 15 March 2011); U.S. Central Intelligence Agency, World Fact Book, "Southwest Asia: Afghanistan," https://www.cia.gov/library/publications/the-world-factbook/geos/af.html (accessed 15 March 2011).

[52]Sandholtz and Koetzle, 43; Swaleheen and Stansel, 348-352; Candidate 40801, 14; Kwabena Gyimah-Brempong, "Corruption, Economic Growth, and Income Inequality in Africa," *Economics of Governance* 3 (2002), 191; Treisman, 410-427.

[53]Mauro, 681-712.

[54]Ibid., 705-706.

[55]Gyimah-Brempong, 183-209.

[56]Ibid., 207.

[57]Jani Saastamoinen, "Wealth Distribution and Economic Growth" (Discussion Papers #41, University of Joensuu, Finland, October 2006), http://epublications.uef.fi/ pub/urn_isbn_952-458-871-4/urn_isbn_952-458-871-4.pdf (accessed 29 November 2011), 6-22.

[58]Ibid., 25.

[59]Treisman, 399-457.

[60]Ibid., 402.

[61]Ibid., 430.

[62]Ibid.

[63]Sandholtz and Koetzle, 35-36.

[64]Ibid., 42-46.

[65]Ibid., 37-40.

[66]Ibid., 47-48.

[67]Kutan, Douglas, and Judge, 7-9.

[68]Ibid., 9-13.

[69]Ibid., 14-16.

[70]Mushfiq Swaleheen and Dean Stansel, "Economic Freedom, Corruption, and Growth," *Cato Journal* 27, no. 3 (Fall 2007): 343-358.

[71]Ibid., 346.

[72]Ibid., 347.

[73]Ibid., 353.

[74]Leff, 314.

[75]Swaleheen and Stansel, 354.

[76]Robert Klitgaard, *Controlling Corruption* (Berkeley, CA: University of California Press, 1988), 24, 30.

[77]Ibid., 25.

[78]Ibid., 24, 30.

[79]Werner, 200.

[80]Leff, 314; Huntington, 253; Klitgaard, 42.

[81]Klitgaard, 75.

[82]Ibid., 74-91.

[83]Ibid., 183-189.

[84]Ibid., 188.

[85]Ibid., 189.

[86]Daniel Kaufman, "Corruption: The Facts," *Foreign Policy* no. 107 (Summer 1997): 114-130.

[87]Ibid., 119.

[88]Ibid., 115.

[89]Ibid., 122.

[90]Ibid., 124.

[91]Ibid., 126.

[92]David A. Chaikin, "Controlling Corruption by Heads of Government and Political Elites," in *Corruption and Anticorruption*, ed Peter Larmour and Nick Wolanin (Canberra, ACT: Asia Pacific Press, 2001), 97-99.

[93]Chaikin, 102.

[94]Ibid., 112-116.

[95]Ibid., 100.

[96]Ibid.

[97]Ibid., 117.

[98]Zoe Pearson, "An International Human Rights Approach to Corruption," in *Corruption and Anticorruption*, ed Peter Larmour and Nick Wolanin (Canberra, ACT: Asia Pacific Press, 2001), 30-61.

[99]Rose-Ackerman, 368.

[100]Pearson, 49.

[101]Ian S. Livingston, Heather Messera, and Michael O'Hanlan, "Afghanistan Index: Tracking Variable of Reconstruction & Security in Post-9/11 Afghanistan," http://www.brookings.edu/afghanistanindex (accessed 15 March 2011).

[102]Integrity Watch Afghanistan, "Afghan Perceptions and Experiences of Corruption" (National Survey 2010), http://www.iwaweb.org/corruptionSurvey2010/NationalCorruption2010.html (accessed 15 March 2011).

[103]U.S. Government Accountability Office, *Afghanistan: Key Issues for Congressional Oversight*, April 2009, http://www.gao.gov/new.items/d09473sp.pdf (accessed 14 November 2011).

[104]U.S. Government Accountability Office. *Contract Management: DOD Vulnerabilities to Contracting Fraud, Waste, and Abuse*, 7 July 2006, http://www.goa.gov/products/GAO-06-838R (accessed 21 September 2011).

CHAPTER 3

RESEARCH DESIGN

The analyses will draw upon case studies, empirical research, survey responses, and data analyses of corruption levels relative to gross domestic product (GDP). The results will determine which theoretical works or empirical assessments best apply for the examination of corruptions effects on Afghanistan's development. The study will relate transnational scholarly studies that closely correlate to the conditions in Afghanistan as a primary focus. Interviewed sources will provide confirmation to the data and theoretical application assessments.

The *Integrity Watch Afghanistan* report, Government Accountability Office reports, and *Brookings Institution* report are the measuring basis to determine the actual effects and perceptions of corruption in Afghanistan by the population.[1] These reports are the foundation from which the study will extrapolate the impacts of corruption in Afghanistan. Supporting information will come from an interview with a local Afghan officer and other military officers recently exposed to conditions in Afghanistan. The Afghan officer will also serve as a sounding board for recommendations drawn from anti-corruption material to determine the likelihood of acceptance.

The empirical studies of corruption by Mauro, Treisman, Sandoltz, Kutan, and Swaleheen all indicate that corruption has negative impacts on foreign and domestic investment that reduces economic development.[2] These studies also indicate that corruption contributes to instability and inefficiency. These scholars all use the corruption perception index to evaluate correlations to corruption and other factors in economic development and stability. These different connections associate capital accumulation and flight, governance structures, and social development and integration capacities to corruption levels. These studies provide correlations to the levels of corruption to economic, stability indicators, and other factors that exist or may develop in Afghanistan. These works will also provide potential indirect routes to reduce corruption in conjunction with an anti-corruption policy.

Nye's study examines the probability of corruption benefiting development and the relationship cultural practices have to activities associated with corruption.[3] This study indicates that most corruption is detrimental to development but there are limited conditions where corruption can facilitate growth. Huntington's study offers corruption as an unavoidable byproduct of cultural development. This will serve as a reference of timing anti-corruption efforts as well as understanding for corruptions existence apart from immediate cultural associations.

Leff's theories offer rationale for cases of corruption benefitting cultural growth. The theories of corruption considered are the potential for overcoming cumbersome bureaucratic procedures and government leadership with little interest in cultural development.[4] Bribery in these theories justify payments to government employees and social elites as a means of cutting through red tape that delay government processes or to provide incentives for social elites to consider options outside of the norms that are keeping them in power. The most powerful effect this argument presents is that bribery can serve to establish trust with outsiders by demonstrating a form of buy-in from the outsider. Corruption also has potential for effective competition and efficiency.[5] The consideration is that corruption could serve as a non-official method for executing functions managed by a mature government system. Examples of these functions would

41

be taxation and wealth consolidation. The theory also suggests that bribes serve as a means of prioritizing the allocations of scarce resources to those willing to pay more and to provide motivation for government employee productivity when the central government lacks the funds for sufficient salaries. If the analysis demonstrates a positive effect to the economy despite corrupt behavior, then Leff's theories would be useful in justifying a policy of noninterference.

The corruption theories of Rose-Ackerman provide contrast to the benefits presented by Leff. Rose-Ackerman states that corruption reduces efficiency.[6] Instead of providing an incentive and priority to the person willing to pay the bribe to the under-paid government agent, it makes bribe payment a requirement by all to receive a service and has further costs in keeping the elicit transaction a secret. Further arguments against efficiency reduce competition. This contradicts Leff's theory that the most efficient businesses are those capable and willing to pay the higher bribe for a contract. Corrupt businesses bind themselves to a current regime.[7] This limits information shared regarding contract availability or consideration to outside businesses. This creates monopolies amongst the cultural elites and facilitates capital flight. These considerations fail to integrate a society and foster economic development. These theories provide indicators for corruption having a negative effect on economic development.

Heidenheimer's theory of graying corruption is applicable when corruption exists in a culture.[8] This theory will be considered when determining what act likely had some benefit. Heidenheimer's discussion of the deterioration of the occasional acts to persistent and destructive corrupt practices may uncover reasons why the corruption has become such a problem in Afghanistan.[9] Werner's study of Israel also presents a valid condition

42

where corruption has a lifecycle. Werner's study indicates that corruption will not naturally end, nor absolutely driven from a country.[10] These theorists provide both urgency and realistic expectations for an anti-corruption policy as well as rationale for greater scrutiny on indicators that may be misleading.

The studies of Tornell and Benhabib outline the social and political games conducted within developing cultures.[11] The games provide rationale behind why cultural elites take actions to hide wealth they accumulate from others. These games involve capital flight and explain why the country's economy declines despite foreign aid. Tanzi's work on the social impacts of corruption explains the impacts and justifications for nepotism.[12]

Transnational comparisons from the studies of Voskanyan, and Gyimah-Brempong provide case studies on the impacts of corruption on states.[13] Voscanyan's study provides information regarding mental barriers in a society's ability to deviate from corrupt behavior that has long taken root in a government.[14] This information is useful in understanding the pace for anti-corruption activities. Gyimah-Brempong's African study shows the impact corruption has had on development, particularly with bribers and misappropriation of government funds. This information will be useful in assessing the effects of U.S. funding in stability operations.

Anti-corruption guidance from Klitgaard, Pearson, Chaikin and Kaufmann all provide methods for improving corruption levels within a country. Klitgaard's work serves as a handbook for developing an anti-corruption program as well as examples where cultural norms were challenges and changed within acceptable cultural means.[15] Pearson offers a solution from a human right perspective.[16] Chaikin identifies legal and

43

privacy rights problems that facilitate corruption.[17] Kaufmann confirms many of the

empirical studies that demonstrate corruptions negative effects and identifies external

factors that justify a larger perspective for anti-corruption efforts beyond a simple focus

on Afghanistan.[18] These works provide options to attack corruption. The combination of

these works will shape the proposed solution for Afghanistan.

Table 1 summarizes the sources and variable factors used in the analyses.

Table 1.    Source and Variable Factors

| Source: | Factor Variable: |
|---|---|
| Integrity Watch Afghanistan | Afghan Perceptions |
| Government Accountability Officer | Monetary Costs and Progress in Afghanistan |
| Brookings Institute | Economic and Stability Results |
| Mauro, Treisman, Kutan, Sandholtz, and Swaleheen | Economic Correlations to Corruption |
| Nye | Corruption Cost-Benefit Analyses and Probabilities |
| Leff | Benefits of Corruption |
| Rose-Ackerman | Costs of Corruption |
| Heidenheimer | Graying Theory |
| Werner | Corruption Life Cycle |
| Tornell and Benhabib | Capital Flight |
| Voskanyan | Mental and Cultural Barriers to Change |
| Gyimah-Brempong | Economic Costs to Foreign Aid |
| Klitgaard | Anti Corruption Policy and Successes |
| Pearson | Human Rights Perspective |
| Chaikin | Legal Changes in Privacy Rights |
| Kaufmann | External Influencers |

*Source*: Created by author.

---

[1]Integrity Watch Afghanistan, "Afghan Perceptions and Experiences of Corruption," *National Survey* 2010, http://www.iwaweb.org/corruptionSurvey2010/ NationalCorruption2010.html (accessed 15 March 2011); Livingston, Messera, and O'Hanlan.

[2]Mauro, 681-712; Treisman, 399-457; Sandholtz and Koetzle, 31-50; Kutan and Douglas, 1-14; Swaleheen and Stansel, 343-358.

[3]Nye, 417-427.

[4]Leff, 312-313.

[5]Ibid., 313-315.

[6]Rose-Ackerman, 357-360.

[7]Ibid., 361-366.

[8]Heidenheimer, 141-154.

[9]Ibid.

[10]Werner, 199-220.

[11]Tornell and Velasco, 1208-1231; Benhabib and Rustichini, 125-142.

[12]Tanzi, 161-181.

[13]Voskanyan, 1-26; Gyimah-Brempong, 183-209.

[14]Voskanyan, 17.

[15]Klitgaard, 181-189.

[16]Pearson, 30-61.

[17]Chaikin, 97-117.

[18]Kaufman, 114-130.

Chapter 4

ANALYSIS

This chapter analyzes the theoretical considerations for corruption and evidence that support the theories. It then discusses the specific findings in reference to the conditions in Afghanistan. The sequence for this chapter will provide the answers to the secondary questions, on how do Afghans perceive corruption?, In the context of corruption, how is bribery affecting Afghanistan's economic development?, What are U.S. perceptions of the Afghan culture of corruption?, and is U.S. funding affecting corruption and economic development in Afghanistan? The analysis is based on in the knowledge of military officers from Afghanistan, U.S. military officers who have recent experiences in Afghanistan, governmental and non-governmental reports and survey documents taken by sample citizens in Afghanistan.

The interviews of U.S. officers and an Afghan officer enhance the understanding of the environment of Afghanistan through firsthand experience. The analysis utilizes an interview with Major Ryan Bulger who returned from Afghanistan in 2011. His account involves an investigation into corrupt activity in his sector. Major Joseph Coolman, a civil affairs officer, witnessed the results of corrupt government interfering with incentives for foreign investment. The last referenced interview is from a senior Afghan military specialist who is a subject matter expert regarding direct and historical impacts of corruption in his country. This individual is Subject 1 for purposes of anonymity.

<u>How do Afghans perceive corruption?</u>

The Afghans associate corruption as a byproduct of a weak accountability system, low civil servant salaries, and large sums of money in circulation.[1] Figure 1 depicts the full range of responses, from a 2007 survey of 6500 Afghans spread across thirteen provinces on their association of the causes of bribery.

# DUE TO COPYRIGHT RESTRICTIONS SOME OR ALL IMAGES ARE NOT INCLUDED

Figure 1.   Causes of Corruption
*Source:* Integrity Watch Afghanistan, "Afghan Perceptions and Experiences of Corruption," *National Survey 2010*, http://www.iwaweb.org/corruptionSurvey2010/ NationalCorruption2010.html (accessed 15 March 2011), 42.

The majority of these perceived causes indicate a lack of punishment by the government and enforcement agencies upon those involved in corrupt activity. This observation minimizes legitimate opportunities to address corrupt behavior. The low salaries for government employees provide an excuse for government agents to seek a bribe or supplemental payments, as well as a rationale for public sympathy and acceptance for bribe solicitation. The lack of monitoring and enforcement, indicated by lines one and four through eight, also facilitate corruption. These listed factors demonstrate a reduced accountability by the government and its employees.

The majority of the Afghan responses in the *Integrity Watch Afghanistan* report associate corruption with the act of bribery. In addition, many other professional articles, such as those from Leff, Rose-Ackerman, and Gyimah-Brempong, discussing the impacts of corruption focus on the act of bribery. Bribery is only one aspect of corruption, but is the easiest act to assign a numerical cost and to associate with illicit activity. The aspect of human nature that drives corruption into a downward spiral is greed.[2] Bribery is not a widespread cultural norm in Afghanistan, since ninety percent of Afghans felt guilty about paying bribes.[3] Given the large sentiment that bribery is wrong, why is it so frequent?

The democratic government in Afghanistan is young and continues to develop the bureaucratic institutions to perform proper accounting.[4] The recent Afghan focus on corruption has magnified the negative opinion regarding it and desire for corrective action. In 2007, the Afghan perception regarding corruption was negative from a moral and religious standpoint, but, in 2010, the perception developed to an abuse of office. The most conservative viewpoints consider corruption as treasonous against the state.[5]

The inevitable and constant presence of corruption in all nations represents the process of growth and transition, as expressed by Huntington.[6] In more advanced cultures, laws establish limitations and guidelines for behavior. The people demand these laws to increase visibility and accountability. Economically developed cultures have the assets to monitor and enforce these rules. Such monitored activities include lobbying and electoral campaign contributions.[7]

Huntington further states that underdeveloped countries do not have the same structured laws that govern behavior of the public servant.[8] Underdeveloped governments also tend not to have the resources to maintain a functional bureaucratic system to monitor and enforce these laws. Corrupt activity is the most common practice for how government and people interact in Afghanistan.[9] As government institutions become stronger, Huntington predicts that people will start to change their expectations of those in power and will drive for more of the laws that reduce corruption.

Some Afghans feel that corruption, particularly bribery, fuels insurgency. They report rumors or beliefs that the Taliban want to fight the government on grounds of corruption.[10] Major Bulger discussed how the Taliban have more integrity in the eyes of the Afghan people than the local national government.[11] This is because the Taliban provide receipts for fees, unlike the police and military. Such receipts, even if they represent protection payments or taxes, are used by the people to show other members of the Taliban and prevent further collection of a tax. This may indicate why there is growing support for the Taliban. Although the Taliban have an unfavorable rating amongst most Afghans, the disfavor rating declined from 79 to 68 percent between 2005 and 2010.[12]

Figure 2 shows a reduction of Afghans' perceived problem with corruption's impact on the country. The problem perceived as a "severe impact" has dropped by 29 percent from 2009-2010.[13] The figure indicates the adversity corruption creates between the government of Afghanistan and the public between 2006 through 2010. Figure 2 also

49

shows an increase of corruption viewed as a "moderate impact" by 16 percent and a

"small impact" by 8 percent.[14]

DUE TO COPYRIGHT RESTRICTIONS
SOME OR ALL IMAGES ARE NOT
INCLUDED

Figure 2.   Corruption among Government Officials

*Source:* Ian Livingston, Heather Messera, and Michael O'Hanlan, "Afghanistan Index: Tracking Variable of Reconstruction & Security in Post-9/11 Afghanistan," 28 February 2011, http://www.brookings.edu/afghanistanindex (accessed 15 March 2011), 38.

The perceived improvement of corruption as a problem in the government could

indicate that the anti-corruption initiatives implemented by the coalition and Afghan

government are meeting with some success. Examples of initiatives sponsored by the

United States Agency for International Development are the High Office of Oversight,

Capacity Development Program Office, and the Afghanistan Rule of Law Program.

These education programs publicize expectations of the government and for newly

established anti-corruption agencies. Additional capabilities for reporting corrupt activity

in the courts system have enabled enforcement of the rule of law.[15] In August 2010, the military established the Combined Joint Interagency Task Force-Shafafiyat.[16] This task force's purpose is to develop a common understanding of corruption, to support Afghan-led anti-corruption effort, and to integrate ISAF anti-corruption activities with those of key partners.[17]

Although there appears to be progress in reducing the impacts or perceptions of corruption, there is an equal potential for Afghans to become more accepting to corrupt practices. The theory of "graying corruption," as described by Heidenheimer, highlights degradation of moral standards.[18] This could be a possibility due to the long period of exposure the country has had to corruption within the highest levels of government.

Figure 3 maps the perceptions that Afghans have had over the last six years on the direction the national government's legitimacy.

DUE TO COPYRIGHT RESTRICTIONS
SOME OR ALL IMAGES ARE NOT INCLUDED

Figure 3.   Afghan Perception of Government Development
*Source:* Ian Livingston, Heather Messera, and Michael O'Hanlan, "Afghanistan Index: Tracking Variable of Reconstruction & Security in Post-9/11 Afghanistan," 28 February 2011, http://www.brookings.edu/afghanistanindex (accessed 15 March 2011), 36.

According to figure 3, Afghans believe that the country is heading in the wrong direction. The confidence in the national government's legitimacy has dropped from 70-59 percent in the last year.[19] The 2009 increase to 70 percent is likely in response to the United States' commitment and surge into the country.[20] The timing of this surge correlates directly with the increased legitimacy perception from a 40 percent in 2008.[21] This figure depicts that corruption is not acceptable in the eyes of the Afghans towards the monopoly power of the government and the corruption within it. The large increase in confidence in the government in 2009 seems to indicate that Afghans had belief in the coalition's ability to correct the corruption concerns within the government.

### How is bribery affecting Afghanistan's economic development?

The 2010 United Nations Crime and Corruption report indicated that one out of every two Afghans paid a bribe to public officials in rural and urban communities for that year.[22] These bribes totaled $2.5 billion, approximately one quarter of Afghanistan's gross domestic product (GDP).[23] The excessive frequency and amount of bribes paid by Afghans rules out the probability that the circumstances that bribery may be beneficial exist.

Table 2 depicts the decline of the Afghan economy despite increasing U.S. financial support between 2005 and 2010. The 2009 U.S. Government Accountability Office report lists annual funding from the U.S. to the Afghan government for governance support, security and reconstruction has increased over time and measured in the millions of dollars.[24] The corruption perception index (CPI) indicates a drastic decline in value and therefore an increase in corrupt activity.[25] The corruption index score dropped over 1 point on a 10-point scale. GDP growth has fallen from 14.5 percent to 8.2

percent, while inflation has risen from 8.4 percent to 20.7 percent.[26]

Table 2.    Annual Economic Changes and U.S. Funding

| Afghanistan | 2005 | 2006 | 2007 | 2008 | 2009 | 2010 |
|---|---|---|---|---|---|---|
| CPI | 2.5 | 2.5 | 1.8 | 1.5 | 1.3 | 1.4 |
| GDP Growth | 14.5 | 11.2 | 11.1 | 3.4 | 20.9 | 8.2 |
| Inflation | 8.4 | 2.4 | 13.2 | 19.6 | 13.3 | 20.7 |
| US Aid to Afghan Governance in $Million | 4,896 | 3,526 | 10,045 | 5,997 | 9,680 | X |

*Source*: Developed by author utilizing Transparency International, "Corruption Perceptions Index, 2010," http://www.transparency.org/policy_research/ surveys_indices/cpi/ (accessed 15 August 2011); U.S. Government Accountability Office, "Afghanistan: Key Issues for Congressional Oversight," April 2009, http://www.gao.gov/new.items/d09473sp.pdf (accessed 14 November 2011), 4; World Bank, http://search.worldbank.org/data?qterm=afghanistan%20GDP%20 growth&language=EN (accessed 15 August 2011); Central Intelligence Agency, World Fact Book, "Southwest Asia: Afghanistan," https://www.cia.gov/library/publications/the-world-factbook/geos/af.html (accessed 15 August 2011).

Corruption hinders growth in Afghanistan. Empirical studies associate a reduction

in growth potential, measured in GDP growth, by 75 to 90 percent per unit of corruption

perception index (CPI).[27] The data in Table 2 indicates that the CPI for Afghanistan has

dropped a total of 1.1 points from a rating of 2.5 in 2005 to a rating of 1.4 by 2010.[28]

GDP growth has fallen from 14.5 percent in 2005 to 8.2 in 2010. This is a decline of 6.3

percent. This decline, averaged over 5 years, is a drop of 1.26 per year (6.3 percent/5

years).[29] Based on the Gyimah-Brempong empirical model, corruption has reduced the

GDP growth of Afghanistan by 87 percent (1.1/1.26).[30] This confirms previous studies measuring corruption's affect on economic growth and the determination that corruption is harmful to development.

Voskanyan associates similar conclusions to the negative impact of corruption on development. Voskanyan explains that corruption increases when a corrupt government receives foreign aid to enhance stability and growth.[31] The increased funding for reconstruction also has a negative effect on Afghanistan. Corruption increases the inequality of wealth distribution.[32] Dishonest, self-serving, or weak willed political leaders consolidate the country's wealth under the obfuscation afforded by corruption and use it to increase their own wealth and power. This increase of political elite's wealth is a result of promoting the government sector relative to the private sector with irresponsible government aid.[33] Afghanistan experiences a huge inflation spike as well as a rise in corruption each year following an increase of funding. The only outlying year appears to be 2009, but this period potentially correlates with the military surge of forces and the increased awareness and effort to reduce corruption.[34] The surge and deliberate anti-corruption effort could also explain the .1 increase from Table 2 in the CPI from a rating of 1.3 in 2009 to a rating of 1.4 in 2010.[35]

Figure 4 lists the individuals that most often participate in acts of bribery as intermediaries. This list is derived from a 2007 survey of 6,500 Afghans spread across thirteen provinces on their association of the causes of bribery. It also shows change in responses to the same question in 2010.

DUE TO COPYRIGHT RESTRICTIONS
SOME OR ALL IMAGES ARE NOT INCLUDED

Figure 4.    Intermediaries in Bribery

*Source:* Integrity Watch Afghanistan, "Afghan Perceptions and Experiences of Corruption," *National Survey 2010*, http://www.iwaweb.org/corruptionSurvey2010/ NationalCorruption2010.html (accessed 15 March 2011), 45.

This figure shows a rise in the unofficial position of the "commissionkar" as well an increase in this person's involvement in bribery.[36] This unofficial position further hides the transaction between two parties to avoid direct proof that the receiver had any action with the person giving the bribe. Typically, activities that result in job development are economically beneficial; this particular job of "commissionkar" negatively affects development. The position adds another set of untraceable hands that cuts into the profits of the final recipient and increases the size of the bribe demanded.

The formation of this position supports scholarly examinations of the social games played by societal elites. These games involve utilizing the secretive nature of corruption to shift wealth and money away from the potential hands of competitors in order to maintain power and advantage over each other.[37] Because of these actions, resources are wasted and moved out of the country. Social games result in the capital flight that causes the severe damage to economic development, since development hinges on the ability to create wealth.

Other effects of a country's wealth are the development of a labor force and the attraction of foreign investment. Corruption negatively affects foreign investment and work force development.[38] The highest bribes paid are for basic social services, such as for education and health, as well as bribes for simple employment.[39] The need to pay large sums of money for education inhibits the average Afghan's ability to get trained and educated. Corruption also reduces the value of training and education, because skills obtained through these measures do not provide a decisive basis for employment. This lack of workforce development further restricts economic growth in Afghanistan.

Major Coolman discussed an experience where corruption dissuaded a potential foreign investor from aiding a province in Iraq.[40] A private investor was willing to establish electrical distribution. The investor planned to pay all the costs to emplace the needed power generation and supply lines to Kirkuk. The first ten years would be at the expense of the investor, with the following ten years he would provide services at cost. The investor and Kirkuk province leaders agreed to renegotiate new terms after the first twenty years. The approved contract halted at the Minister of Energy level.[41] The contractor told Major Coolman that the Minister only would approve the contract under the condition that he would receive the salaries of four fictitious workers at the rate of $20,000 per year.[42]

In the scenario described by Major Coolman, bribery halted economic development since the investor refused to agree to the terms of approval. Even though this experience is from Iraq, Subject 1 indicates that this corrupt activity is similar in Afghanistan to make logical connections.[43] This observation negates Leff's theory that the most skilled laborer or contractor will pay the most for the job best suited for him and that it fosters competition for the most efficient contract.[44] In this circumstance, no contractor replaced this one and he did not pay the bribe despite potential profits. It additionally supports several empirical studies that demonstrate a negative correlation between corruption and foreign investment.

Subject 1 commented the huge increase of money from foreign aid in the area has fostered a mentality of greed. The contractors and the people making and accepting products from contracts make it worse. A contractor acquires a low quality item and stamps a higher quality brand on it. The contractor proceeds to provide the item to the inspector or contracting office. The contracting office accepts the item because he gets a cut of the profit made by the contractors' savings as a bribe. Subject 1 uses body armor as an example. A United Kingdom armor stamped "high quality" was worse than armor made in India. This resulted in the loss of an Afghan soldier's life. A test demonstrated the round fired from a gun went through the substandard armor with the United Kingdom stamp, but did not penetrate the armor from India.[45] This practice affects the quality of life and the safety of Afghan soldiers because this activity occurs with all things from fuel and oil to maintenance parts. This risk transfers to the U.S. Soldier who conduct partnered operations with the Afghan security forces.

The realization that corruption is destroying competitive based efficiency presents a situation where Rose-Ackerman's theory is most applicable.[46] Rose-Ackerman's theory explains the second order effect of "speed money" (bribes paid to cut bureaucratic processes) in the short-run may motivate increased performance, but will result in no

work performed unless the bribe is paid.[47] Corruption's benefits are illusionary.[48] Figure

5 supports this theory and indicates 70 percent of Afghans were certain to highly certain

that the bribe assured the service.

DUE TO COPYRIGHT RESTRICTIONS
SOME OR ALL IMAGES ARE NOT INCLUDED

Figure 5.   Certainty of Bribes to get Government Service

*Source:* Integrity Watch Afghanistan, "Afghan Perceptions and Experiences of
Corruption," *National Survey 2010*, http://www.iwaweb.org/corruptionSurvey2010/
NationalCorruption2010.html (accessed 15 March 2011), 39.

Both figure 5 and Subject 1 affirm that bribes are required for work in a corrupt

government. As an example, government officials require individual Afghans citizens to

buy permits to rebuild their destroyed homes. If the official that was paid changes, then

the new official states the original permit to build is a forgery or expired, and the citizen

must pay again. In order to fight this, one must pay the police, judge, or mayor another

bribe to look into the issue.[49]

Corruption is diminishing the legitimacy of the Afghan government, which in turn

has a negative effect on its economic development.[50] This effect creates further instability and fosters more opportunities for corruption. Instability not only creates risk for investment that exceeds most logical motivations, but also provides incentives for those who currently are in power to accumulate as much personal wealth as possible.

The loss of legitimacy is evident with the lack of faith in the judicial processes. Corruption causes the Afghan people to take judicial matters to non-state actors for resolution. Sixty percent of the 6,500 Afghans across thirty-two provinces responded to the *Integrity Watch Afghanistan* survey that they took judicial matters to non-state actors.[51] Seventy-five percent of these cases were from rural areas, as opposed to the ten percent from towns near cities, and eleven percent from within cities.[52] The 2010 estimate for the population of Afghanistan is nearly thirty million. Seventy-nine percent of Afghans live in the rural areas where non-state actors are preferred over state officials.[53] Confidence in the enforcement and creation of the rule of law are vital to a government's legitimacy. This demonstrated lack of faith reflects the impact corruption is having, especially amongst the institutions designed to fight it.

DUE TO COPYRIGHT RESTRICTIONS
SOME OR ALL IMAGES ARE NOT
INCLUDED

Figure 6. Non-State Justice Providers

*Source:* Integrity Watch Afghanistan, "Afghan Perceptions and Experiences of Corruption," *National Survey 2010*, http://www.iwaweb.org/corruptionSurvey2010/NationalCorruption2010.html (accessed 15 March 2011), 77.

Another indication of the government losing legitimacy is the declining popularity of the President, Hamid Karzai. Brookings poll indicated his popularity fell from 70 to 59 percent between 2009 and 2010.[54] Corruption appears to be a principle cause for this loss of legitimacy. The indicators are the reports of Taliban motivations against the corrupt government, the drop in Taliban disapproval, and former supporters and warlords from the Northern provinces are threatening to establish a formal alliance against the President.[55]

Violence is often the only perceived recourse for those suffering from corruption. Subject 1 emphasizes that there is no legitimate means for the average person with little money to get justice or even simply live season to season. Subject 1 stated the Taliban was first established because of the corruption introduced by the Mujahideen when they overthrew the government in 1992.[56] This indicates that corruption causes the government to lose legitimacy and encourages violence.

Bribery can cause a downward cycle of instability and further corruption. The fear of not conforming to "the publically perceived way of life" keeps people from changing their norms.[57] The resignation of Afghanistan's central bank governor reinforces this theory's application. The governor resigned and fled to America for fear of his life when the unwilling government refused to further investigate and prosecute people involved with the Kabul Bank scandal.[58]

Even though the frequency of bribery is high, there is still the possibility that there could be economic benefit for the country. Major Bulger discussed the lack of government funding to develop regional areas and lack of bureaucratic process to officially tax tribes to pay for services needed.[59] If the monies collected served as a method for wealth consolidation, and are ultimately used towards the benefit of the local population, then bribery would serve as a replacement for the bureaucratic process of taxation.

According to Subject 1, this potential for wealth-consolidation does not serve the needs for people in power to fulfill their duties.[60] Subject 1 says, "All the monies received through bribes are for personal use and power gain."[61] The money exchanges hands up the authoritarian chain and each person take his cuts. People, like the aviation commander from Major Bulger's interview, seek lucrative positions that can extort bribes and pay for them with bribes to whatever higher authority can provide the job. The chain of command receives regular bribe payments for these positions.

When asked about the Afghan government's ability to collect taxes, Subject 1 said that it does have a tax system. However, the system is also corrupt and inefficient in accountability. Most of the money collected does not get to the official government. The officials charged with carrying out duties for the government siphon the funds to their personal purses.[62] Subject 1 uses an example where $50,000 is the fee, but only $20,000 is collected.[63] The businessperson saves $30,000, the taxman makes $20,000, and pays some of that to get away with it.[64] The government bureaucrats take a share of money for the people each level down. Each level takes some of the money for itself before giving it out.[65]

A corrupt climate drives individuals to make financial gains wherever possible. Government employees, such as military personnel, have access to property that is not available to the populous as a whole. This provides individuals with material they can leverage to draw income. In Western culture, the unauthorized use of these materials is misappropriation, which is a subset of corruption.

An example of misappropriation in Afghanistan is the use of military helicopters to transport politicians across the country.[66] This is as a result of a need of the social elite to move safely and quickly across the country. By Western standards, the use of government equipment for personal profit is a misuse of government equipment. However, this act of misappropriation provided a service the government did not have established. This circumstance does provide potential for supporting Leff's theory that corruption increased utility of the aircraft and the associated bribes provided prioritization for seating.[67] The higher the need to fly would result in a higher bribe payment.

Major Bulger commented that the Afghan commander endorsing these flights would cancel Afghan soldier's leave if someone had paid for a seat.[68] This reemphasizes Subject 1's point that greed drives decisions and ultimately hurts those who cannot pay the bribes. Subject 1 states that most acts of misappropriation are simple acts of theft. Subject 1 uses an example of proper sand-to-concrete mixes used for construction. He indicates that instead of using the standard 3:1 sand-to-concrete mix, the person in control of the concrete will steal one bag to sell and change the mix to 6:1.[69] The same occurs with anything that is under the control of the leader. The contractor then either uses the concrete for himself or makes money selling it.[70]

Subject 1 tells of an act of misappropriation that further demonstrates that misappropriation has the same impacts with bribery. Subject 1 uses the example of the Taliban's murder of Ahmed Wali Karzai, brother to the Afghan President to show that violence and instability are a result of corruption.[71] Ahmed's position allowed him to buy several thousand acres of government land that he later sold back to the people and other businesses for a considerable profit.[72] This kind of activity delegitimizes the government and further provokes the Taliban and other disgruntled people to resort to acts of violence.

The large public outcry against bribery further indicates that the monies paid in bribes have not resulted in economic growth for a community, especially because most of the monies collected through bribery are not serving in the tax collection capacity. This would support several scholars' observations of the harmful impacts of corruption.

<u>What are U.S. perceptions of the Afghan</u>
<u>culture of corruption?</u>

Great military leaders such as General Petraeus have the insight and

understanding for cultural considerations. In his initial entrance into Iraq, he knew that to

impose a U.S. solution to a problem would not be an effective answer for an acceptable

solution.[73] General Petraeus's insights shaped lessons dealing with counterinsurgency.

Counterinsurgency is the principle U.S. operation in Afghanistan. Corruption appears to

be fostering insurgent activity in Afghanistan. Training exercises in preparation for

advising foreign police and military forces emphasized consideration for the culture and

not imposing the American answer to solve host nation problems. However, despite the

training and understanding, literature indicates that Western cultures lack understanding

or at least patience in dealing with underdeveloped cultures.

As examples, the U.S. military identify corrupt practices in Afghanistan and Iraq

as a cultural norm that must be accepted in order to generate results within the span of a

deployment. This is particularly the case with nepotism. Identifying and accepting tribal

practices is easier for the U.S. military than to analyze and explain how and why

nepotism amongst the tribes exist, and then to educate tribes on the consequences of

nepotism and advantages of change and evolution. Tribes formed out of the need for

social integration and development. Tribal formation occurred over many years. Further

development requires more emphasis on expansion and integration. However, these

forms of development are hard to measure or quantify, especially when soldiers focus on

identifying progress in the short tenure of a deployment.

Vito Tanzi provides insights regarding the social implications of this type of

culture.[74] The practice of nepotism and trading in favors are dominant in cultures that hold more value in strong family bond and loyalty over society's growth. Afghanistan has a tribal system that places this same emphasis on importance of the family over society as a whole.[75] In knowing this, contract projects hire local people and tribes. Hiring local people enhances efforts to provide income and employment for poor people. There is also a general impression that violence will occur otherwise, e.g. projects that will suffer from sabotage or attacks by the local people, reinforcing the U.S. notion that unskilled workers must come locally for a development contract to be successful.[76]

Subject 1 stated that hiring of local workers for contracts is not necessary. The tribes just want to get their share of the large sums of foreign aid and project money in circulation in Afghanistan. They will cause trouble for the contractor unless their tribe members are hired or unless the contractor pays a bribe. The contractor chooses who to hire as labor between stipulations in the U.S. contract and how much he must bribe, because both increase costs for contracts. However, Subject 1 stated that people do not share monies from bribes and contracts with their family.[77]

This indicates a shift in mentality from tribal benefit to personal greed. Corruption is degrading in tribal integrity. This lack of commitment violates the communal reason for tribal formation. Tribes are composed of individuals of similar background and lineage. Afghanistan is a conglomeration of several tribes and each tribe claims territory that represents nearly a sovereign territory of itself. Each member of the tribe contributes to the betterment of the whole tribe. This change also indicates that greed has become a more deeply rooted factor in Afghan culture. This condition reflects the consequences of Heidenheimer's "graying" effects on corruption.[78] Nepotism negatively affects the hiring of individuals based on competency, it hurts development and incentives for education

65

and pursuing needed skills.[79] The lack of desire of the people to get skills and the government is removing any ability to excel on merit are the most severe costs of nepotism.

The culture therefore is blamed for the lack of achieving quick and tangible effects. As a result, contract requirements and local area project planning considerations make deliberate efforts to identify and include local tribe members to be the unskilled labor force. The influx of money into Afghanistan influences these non-economic based decisions. This money has opened opportunities for greed and cultural moral degradation. Each Afghan knows that there is a large amount of money available and the people, even at the most uneducated level, want to get their share of it. Americans desire to show tangible results for their efforts there result in accepting corrupt behavior in order to achieve them.

> Military spending on a contractor force that exceeded the number of troops deployed led to massive waste, gross inflation of prices, a pervasive climate of corruption, and abuses like struggles between power brokers and tolerance of the payment of protection money to the Taliban. This vastly increased the cost of the war, seriously hurt the regular Afghan economy, and damaged the reputation of the Afghan Government (GIROA) and its popular support.[80]

Rose-Ackerman states that the costs of the bribery transfer to unproductive cuts in material or added costs to the population.[81] This discredits bribery as a means of efficiently selecting skilled workers or promoting competition. From personal observations, the author witnessed the impacts of poor oversight and bribery on U.S. contracts in Iraq, where a contract was developed to build a headquarters and training facility for an Iraqi signal intercept company. The contract was for a building for the new units, including precise technical considerations. U.S. engineers created the contract that had all the requirements correct and funding to fulfill the projects needs, but after layers of subcontracting, only part of the project started before the funding had disappeared and the project came to a grinding halt. The Iraqi division commander commented in a leader engagement with the author that he could not move more troops onto the base until the project was completed. The author learned that there was substandard batch of concrete that had arrived and had initially been used in the foundation. The delays were a result of a subcontractor bringing the poor concrete and requesting additional funding for correct materials.[82] The contract is one of many casualties of bribery and the effects of this sort of costs on a community.

Subject 1's interview supports the scholarly observations that irresponsible funding of foreign projects only fosters corruption. Subject 1 identifies several organizations that are trying to help the development of villages in Afghanistan, but they only start the money flow. The lack of representation and accountability throughout the process allows for both bribery and misappropriation. In the example provided from Subject 1: "There is no oversight and a lot of money irresponsibly spent into Afghanistan." An NGO or person wanting a contract hires someone for a $1 million dollar job, the contractor then goes to another to do the same job for half that. The job transfers to another sub contractor who ends up with $250,000 to $200,000 to do the job. Then the subcontractor unofficially has to pay the mayor and the tribal leader for permissions to build, then pays the government for the permits to build, He also pays the police and the Taliban for protection. Following these payments, he takes a personal cut. The remainder creates a much smaller project or one that barely pays the worker's salaries and uses poor quality material or inappropriate mixes of cement for example. 3:1 sand to cement becomes 6:1 mix."[83]

An interview with Major Bulger demonstrates the reaction military leaders have when confronting a corruption problem. In this scenario an immediate arrest and detainment was not allowed nor was it an ideal solution. Major Bulger's battalion was to reduce the corrupt activity in his area. The unit conducted partnership operations with an Afghan military unit. This Afghan unit accepted bribes from local politicians for military flights to fly them across the country. The bribe payments were accepted by pilots and flights coordinated by the military commanders. Major Bulger stopped one of the flights and had documented proof and witnesses before apprehending the pilot, who had several hundred dollars in U.S. currency. However, a senior ranking United States' officer, told him to release the pilot and return the money. Major Bulger filed the report of the incident, but nothing came from it. His battalion gave up the emphasis on trying to fight corruption and instead focused on more productive tasks.

Western military culture is aggressive, impatient, and results oriented.[84] Although there is the understanding that the solution must come from the population, Western culture conflicts with the patience needed to effectively execute a program that facilitates cultural growth. This impatience negatively affects the American understanding and resourcing of education teaching culture. The military values results. Each commander must show results. As a result, several well-intended and useful projects started and progressed; however, with so many threats and operations executed in Afghanistan, aggressive monitoring and attention to corrupt behavior has suffered. Such a short-term focus helps shape understanding of the "ten, one-year wars" fought in Afghanistan.

## Is U.S. funding affecting corruption and economic development in Afghanistan?

The answer to this question uses a summary of the findings from other secondary questions. Many of the findings will be the source for the conclusions in the following chapter. The common finding is that there are no indicators that corruption provides any benefit to the economic development in Afghanistan.

Since the U.S. increased its emphasis in operations in Afghanistan, corruption has increased. The Corruption Perceptions Index has dropped from 2.5 to 1.4 in the last 5 years.[85] This represents a negative correlation to the near doubling of financial aid provided to Afghanistan from the U.S. government.

Gross Domestic Product in Afghanistan has declined to 8.2 percent from 14 percent over the last 5 years.[86] Popular support for the established government is lower in 2010 than it was in 2004, primarily as a result of the increased corruption within the government.[87] This lack of faith in the government has translated to both an increase in the use of external sources to settle disputes and a reduction in the disfavor seen towards insurgent organizations. As a result, the recent U.S. funding does not demonstrate a positive effect on the Afghan government's legitimacy or to economic development for the country.

The largest potential contributor to this increased perception of corruption is the excessive spending by the United States on contracts.[88] The challenges facing the United States' contracting system center on a failure of adequate contracting expertise and failure to obtain reasonable or adequate prices for services.[89] Following the Government Accountability Office report, the United States developed several organizations to correct these faults. The Army Contracting Command was established in 2008 in order to address the systemic problems with contracting.[90] The Special Inspector General for Afghanistan

Reconstruction is conducting audits on all projects that have been executed in

Afghanistan and actively monitors the usage of the Commander's Emergency Relief

Program and Trouble Asset Relief Programs.[91] These efforts, coupled with the

aforementioned Combined Joint Interagency Task Force-Shafafiyat, all indicate a more

determined, deliberate, and long term vision to advance stability in Afghanistan.

---

[1]Integrity Watch Afghanistan, 13.

[2]Ibid.

[3]Ibid., 14.

[4]United States Agency for International Development: Afghanistan, *Assessment of Corruption in Afghanistan* (Washington, DC: Government Printing Office, 2009), http://pdf.usaid.gov/pdf_docs/PNADO248.pdf (29 November 2011), 2-3.

[5]Ibid., 40.

[6]Huntington, 254.

[7]Federal Election Commission, "The FEC and the Federal Campaign Finance Law," February 2010, http://www.fec.gov/pages/brochures/fecfeca.shtml# Contribution_Limits (accessed 17 September 2011).

[8]Huntington, 254.

[9]Subject 1, Interview.

[10]Integrity Watch Afghanistan, 11.

[11]Bulger, Interview.

[12]Livingston, Messera, and O'Hanlan, 37.

[13]Ibid., 38.

[14]Ibid.

[15]United States Agency for International Development, Afghanistan, 2-3.

[16]U.S. Government Accountability Office. "Progress Toward Security and Stability in Afghanistan," Report to Congress, November 2010, www.defense.gov/pubs/November_1230_Report_FINAL.pdf (accessed 18 May 2011), 10.

[17]Ibid.

[18]Heidenheimer, 141-154.

[19]Livingston, Messera, and O'Hanlan, 36.

[20]U.S. Government Accountability Office, "Progress Toward Security and Stability in Afghanistan," 11.

[21]Livingston, Messera, and O'Hanlan, 36.

[22]United Nations Office on Drugs and Crime, 4.

[23]Ibid.

[24]U.S. Government Accountability Office, *Afghanistan: Key Issues for Congressional Oversight*, 4.

[25]Transparency International.

[26]World Bank, http://search.worldbank.org/data?qterm=afghanistan%20GDP%20growth&language=EN (accessed 15 August 2011); U.S. Central Intelligence Agency, "Southwest Asia: Afghanistan."

[27]Gyimah-Brempong, 207; Mauro, 700-705; Treisman, 417-418.

[28]Transparency International.

[29]World Bank; U.S. Central Intelligence Agency,World Fact Book, "Country Comparison: GDP," https://www.cia.gov/library/publications/the-world-factbook/rankorder/2001rank.html (accessed 15 March 2011)

[30]Gyimah-Brempong, 207.

[31]Voskanyan, 26.

[32]Gyimah-Brempong, 183-209.

[33]Voskanyan, 26.

[34]U.S. Government Accountability Office, "Progress Toward Security and Stability in Afghanistan."

[35]Transparency International.

[36] Integrity Watch Afghanistan, 45.

[37] Jess Benhabib and Aldo Rustichini, 125-142; Tornell and Velasco, 1208-1231.

[38] Sandholtz, 37-40.

[39] Integrity Watch Afghanistan, 12.

[40] Major Joseph Coolman, U.S. Army, L202 Class notes from discussion, 6 July 2011.

[41] Ibid.

[42] Ibid.

[43] Subject 1, Interview.

[44] Leff, 314.

[45] Subject 1, Interview.

[46] Rose-Ackerman, 357.

[47] Ibid.

[48] Kaufmann, 115.

[49] Subject 1, Interview.

[50] Nye, 426.

[51] Integrity Watch Afghanistan, 12.

[52] Ibid., 78.

[53] World Food Programme, Population and Demography, http://foodsecurityatlas.org/afg/country/socioeconomic-profile/introduction (accessed 1 October 2011).

[54] Livingston, Messera, and O'Hanlan, 36.

[55] The Economist, "Rough Riding: The Country's Tricky Politics get ever Trickier" 400, no. 8740 (July 2011): 34.

[56] Subject 1, Interview.

[57] Voskanyan, 18.

[58] The Economist, 34.

[59]Bulger, Interview.

[60]Subject 1, Interview.

[61]Ibid.

[62]Ibid.

[63]Ibid.

[64]Ibid.

[65]Ibid.

[66]Bulger, Interview.

[67]Leff, 314.

[68]Bulger, Interview.

[69]Subject 1, Interview.

[70]Ibid.

[71]Ibid.

[72]Ibid.

[73]Kristen Lundberg, "The Accidental Statesman: General Petraeus and the City of Mosul, Iraq," in U.S. Army Command and General Staff College, *L200 Developing Organizations and Leaders: Advance Sheets and Readings* (Fort Leavenworth, KS: USACGSC, December 2010), 68.

[74]Tanzi, 161-181.

[75]Center for Army Lessons Learned, *Afghan Culture Newsletter* (Fort Leavenworth, KS: Combined Arms Center, Septermber 2010), 74-75.

[76]Small Group 1A, ILE Class discussions, 11-02.

[77]Subject 1, Interview.

[78]Heidenheimer, 139-140.

[79]Tanzi, 171.

[80]Center for Strategic International Studies, "Losing the War by Failing to Resource It and Manage the Resources That Were Provided," 2011, http://csis.org/files/publication/110617_AfghanMetrics.pdf (accessed 21 July 2011).

[81]Rose-Ackerman, 358.

[82]Author's personal experience as MiTT Chief April through July 2010.

[83]Subject 1, Interview.

[84]Geoffrey Parker, *The Military Revolution: Military Innovation and the Rise of the West, 1500-1800*, 2nd ed. (Cambridge, UK: Cambridge University Press, 1988), 2-3, 10.

[85]Transparency International.

[86]World Bank; Central Intelligence Agency, World Factbook, https://www.cia.gov/library/publications/the-world-factbook/geos/af.html, 2009-2010 (accessed 15 August 2011).

[87]Livingston, Messera, and O'Hanlan, 36.

[88]Center for Strategic International Studies, "Losing the War by Failing to Resource It and Manage the Resources That Were Provided," 2011, http://csis.org/files/publication/110617_AfghanMetrics.pdf (accessed 21 July 2011).

[89]U.S. Government Accountability Office, *Contract Management: DOD Vulnerabilities to Contracting Fraud, Waste, and Abuse.*

[90]Army Acquisition Command/ACC, 2008, http://www.acc.army.mil/about (accessed 21 September 2011).

[91]Special Inspector General to Afghanistan Reconstruction, 10th Quarterly Report, 30 January 2011, http://www.sigar.mil/pdf/quarterlyreports/Jan2011/Lowres/Jan2011.pdf (accessed 21 September 2011), 1.

# CHAPTER 5

## CONCLUSIONS AND RECOMMENDATIONS

This chapter provides the overall findings of the research and the acceptance or rejection of the hypotheses made in the first chapter. It will describe the effects of corruption on the economic development of Afghanistan, followed by recommendations for addressing corruption in Afghanistan using the instruments of national power: diplomacy, information, military, and economics. The chapter concludes with recommendations for additional study in order to develop a better understanding of the economic effects of corruption and the feasibility of recommendations.

### Findings

Reject hypothesis 1: Afghans perceive corruption as a normal means of doing business, and that the country has no reason to conform to Western bureaucratic practices.

Reject hypothesis 2: Bribery is the means used as an unofficial tax collection to establish the government wealth and to supplement salaries of government employees by the users of the service provided.

Accept hypothesis 3: The U.S. perceives Afghanistan as a corrupt society and the practices of nepotism and bribery are part of the culture.

Reject hypothesis 4: Funding has a small positive effect on the economic development, whose minimal effects are due to accepting losses from bribery.

Operations in Afghanistan have cost the U.S. over 283 billion dollars.[1] The analysis shows the U.S. has spent 34.1 billion dollars in aid to Afghan governance and development.[2] However, corruption has increased, with a CPI drop of 1.1 on the 10-point

75

scale, growth in GDP has declined 6.3 percent, and inflation has increased 12.3 percent. This problem arose from irresponsible spending on projects and lack of oversight on the monies provided to the Afghan government for developing the country. Afghanistan's problem with bribery and nepotism has contributed to the economic decline despite the foreign aid provided to it.

Afghans do not support bribery, as noted in the surveys, but fail to recognize that nepotism also contributes to the problem of corruption. Both bribery and nepotism reduce growth of GDP since neither practice fosters work force development. Nepotism additionally encourages bribery as a means to overcome tribal or family preferences for employment.

The increase in bribery in the country, as indicated by the increased corruption perceptions of the Afghan population and the decline in the CPI, has decreased the legitimacy of the current Afghan government and increased political instability. Examples previously cited include the 21 percent decline in favor for Hamid Karzai's leadership, the murder of his brother, the flight of the governor of the Kabul Bank, and the change in support of key tribal leaders who once supported President Karzai.

The increased cash in Afghanistan's market, primarily the result of international aid, contributed to the increase in the inflation rates and separated the government and social elites from the people. This increase in cash has multiple effects: It has increased the number of people involved in bribery, modifies the methods contractors in Afghanistan manipulate contracts, increases the amount Afghans must pay in bribes, and explains the appearance of new job of "commissionkar". All of these effects serve to validate theories that foreign aid contribute to increased corruption.[3]

76

## Recommendations

This section provides recommendations to mitigate the problems corruption creates for the development of a country. It also recommends actions to refine foreign financial aid policy to underdeveloped countries. The organization of these recommendations will follow the instruments of government power. The initial recommendations will start with diplomacy, information, military, and close with economic considerations. The recommendations presented in each category will begin with emphasis on Afghanistan, but whose application affect global corruption issues.

Many of the recommendations will overlap and reinforce each other throughout this section. The section on informational power assumes all activities are simultaneous and synchronized. It recognizes that some recommendations may already be in progress, but will reinforce the need for anti-corruption activities and potentially identify linkages between all sources of national power.

### Diplomacy

The following are recommendations for the use of diplomatic power.

1. Identify model leadership for anti-corruption and cultural development and support them through intermediaries.

2. Create an international priority to fight corruption and give it legitimacy.

3. Empower an international body of corruption experts and educators.

The U.S. has identified the current Afghan administration as corrupt and has made several public accusations that Karzai must correct the corruption problem within his country.[4] These accusations have created a rift between the two countries and have limited the ability of the U.S. to influence change in government practice and to develop effective governance policies. The United States' commitment to Afghanistan's development has not led to trust between the states. The U.S. should modify its stance denouncing the leadership as corrupt to promote the trust between the states. However, the extreme corruption in the current Afghan leadership has proven to be detrimental to the country's development.

The United States needs to identify potential Afghan leaders of the country that are against corruption and that have a background relatively free of bribery. The effort to find these potential legitimate leaders should not be constrained to those within the established government. Once found, these individuals should be encouraged to take the responsibility of leadership, trained and developed in creating responsible governance, and publically supported as a model of non-corrupt leadership to the country. The support for the new potential leaders cannot come solely from the U.S. with the current conditions in Afghanistan. The perception of a candidate influenced by the West, affects his legitimacy, his support amongst the people, and neighboring nations' support. The message and support for non-corrupt leaders also needs to come from other respected nations and the media.

In addition to finding and promoting a more legitimate leadership within Afghanistan, there should be efforts to make anti-corruption a global priority. Globalization and constrained resources have challenged developing nation's potential for positive economic growth and stability. Corruption undermines both economic growth and political stability, further threatening the security of all countries. A global anti-corruption policy should be developed and promoted by major international institutions; however, most international institutions lack the authority to enforce their decrees. The development of anti-corruption policies by these institutions should, at a minimum, determine what corrupt practices are. If responsible nations understand the global impacts of corruption, decide to hold each other accountable in good governance practices, and not give any one country the ability to veto or avoid enforcement of the accepted standard, then progress in combating corruption will occur.

The U.S. should sponsor the development of an international body of anti-corruption experts, political and economic experts, and educators to serve as a primary agent to focus on understanding the full impacts of corruption and formulate programs to reduce it. This body should include members from many nations who can provide insight to the various forms of corruption in practice across the world as well as insights on cultural considerations in implementation and acceptance. This panel of experts would focus on best practices for conducting legitimate governance, understanding and discovering corrupt behavior, and expressing the economic and political costs of corruption. They should begin on assisting the government of Afghanistan through forums with government, business, social, and military leaders. With many countries participating in the forum, it is more likely that the government of Afghanistan will be able to find a balance between cultural norms and economic progress that will reduce the amount of corruption. The goal of these forums would be a regular reinforcement that corruption occurs in all societies, exposing its various forms, and how it changes to fit within each different economy. By focusing on these issues, the forums would limit a direct focus on Afghanistan corruption. The findings and understanding gained through these forums would help formulate strategy for attacking corruption on an international level, and further help to demonstrate the importance of addressing corruption on an international level.

## Information

The following are recommendations for the use of information power.

1. Continually reinforce commitment to Afghanistan's stability and development.

2. Share globally the lessons learned from the anti-corruption body.

3. Publicize the success of the international body and the developments of nations fighting corruption.

The U.S. should continue to reinforce its commitment to Afghanistan, notwithstanding the decline of American troops. If Afghanistan feels it is going lose U.S. support, instability will likely result. This instability would be a result of the social elite seeking to secure their position and insurgent forces' taking the opportunity to monopolize the temporary power vacuum. Continued support will also enhance the trust of the people and the government for U.S. intentions.

The information gained by the anti-corruption forums international body, as described above, will provide insight for scholars and governments to help determine standard activities for good governance and economic development. The information and best practices developed by this body must be accessible across the world. The lessons learned from every nation could expose the weaknesses to corruption in any economic system. This information will enable scholars' and leaders' understanding of economic and social conditions and developments through efficient models for management for any society at any stage of development. The use of the information detailing economic consequences and impacts on stability of corruption will educate the Afghan population,

80

especially the cultural elite, and help enhance growth and development of Afghanistan. Sharing this information will further enhance the development of nations and societies beyond Afghanistan.

Chaikin identifies several political elites who were able to steal government funds and left their countries with large debt and little ability to develop.[5] This was possible because of the opacity of corruption and lack of accountability in their countries. The affected countries spread across the globe from the Caucasus, Africa, South America, and the Middle East. These cases of grand corruption are only the high profile cases. Each level of bureaucracy tied to bribery has the ability to chip away at a country's wealth. The U.S. should support globally accepted the best practices and work with governments to develop a culturally acceptable course of action and to publicize its stance against corruption.

The extreme sensitivity to cultural norms in U.S. actions in Afghanistan as noted in the analysis above also undermines the education and mental adaption of U.S. military and civilian leaders in Afghanistan charged with establishing stability in the region. Klitgaard indicates several successful examples for anti-corruption programs, such as in the Philippines, Hong Kong, and Korea.[6] They indicate that fighting corruption is not hopeless and provide examples of successful anti-corruption integration for cultures that do not have a strong institutional baseline or a strong presence of corruption.

Publicizing the successes of this anti-corruption body of experts will further enhance its legitimacy and benefits. The success of this body will also provide global recognition to countries that are successfully reducing corruption. By providing recognition to the countries that are executing meaningful anti-corruption activities, the countries will be further motivated to continue to be a model for progress. They may also be approached by neighboring country leaders on how they achieved their success without directly becoming involved with external support. The notion that all countries desire positive global attention and recognition should motivate a sense of cultural responsibility over individual greed by country leaders.

## Military

The following are recommendations for the use of military power.

1. Adjust focus on long-term development with the understanding that progress may not be measurable within a year.

2. Work closely with external agencies on planning and analysis of conditions for the timing and development of projects.

3. Develop a permanent basing strategy for U.S. forces.

The military must first change the methods by which it measures success. There has been an excessive amount of contracts opened for projects designed to benefit Afghan society. Many projects failed due to sabotage, lack of subcontractor oversight, or a disconnection between the want and needs of the society and the perceived needs by the contracting agents. A slow and deliberate process needs to be adopted in order to facilitate a more economically efficient use of the resources used in the projects and to promote a greater understanding and acceptance of the people who receive the benefits of the project.

This deliberate approach would profit from close-coordination and cooperation among military and civilian agencies. The military is the primary agent executing security and stability operations in Afghanistan. Civilian government agencies, such as

82

USAID, are leading development programs and possess the political and economic expertise to understand the most efficient implementation based on preconditions and synchronization of U.S. efforts. Since corruption directly affects stability, all military operations should support and augment the efforts of agencies of government best suited to identify and enforce legitimate activities.

Currently, the U.S. Army provides flexible and adaptive functions: such as conducting offensive operations against insurgents, training and establishing host nation security forces, providing partnership and mentorship to cultural leaders, and building infrastructure. With current deployment cycles and manning levels, there is a risk that it will lose the expertise in the core competencies involved in high intensity conflicts. However, the military does have unique qualifications to advise and develop the capabilities of the Afghan security forces, which promote the overall goal of Afghan government legitimacy. To advance its commitment to this goal, the U.S. should establish and announce a long-term presence for this "partnership" force, similar to other overseas locations, like Korea. A long-term presence of U.S. military trainers would enhance relationships between Afghan military leaders and provide focus in reducing corruption within the military by way of discussing professional ethics, providing a model of behavior, and offering solutions to local problems.

Economic

The following are recommendations for the use of economic power.

1. Structure foreign aid packages that are conditioned on progress made in reducing corruption.

2. Increase international capabilities to monitor and enforce decrees within its
   designated responsibilities.

3. Refine international banking policies on privacy.

The United States should develop a conditional system of financial aid for countries with high levels of corruption. Aid levels would be based on predetermined levels of corruption using the country's CPI as measured by Transparency International or by other recognized anti-corruption institutions. Some government aid could also be directed to support anti-corruption activities or other factors that contribute to corrupt activities. Such potential conditions should be purposefully variable to allow interpretation by country experts; however, their purpose is to provide financial incentives for a country to make a deliberate effort to affect corruption itself.

The assessment of a country's success in battling corruption should be through the previously recommended body of experts designed to help formulate strategies and educate states on anti-corruption activities. Success would be measured through economic growth and the CPI. This body must be empowered to monitor a country's government bureaucracy in order to determine if positive changes are due to its legitimate efforts. It may be necessary to grant it some degree of authority to encourage cooperation from affected governments.

Reforming privacy and international financial policy must also be emphasized. The secrecy of banking institutions, such as Swiss bank accounts, actually promotes corruption and capital flight.[7] These banking laws are only one example of the types of changes to address internationally. The frequency of corruption among leaders of developing countries, that in turn cripples the economic development of their countries, demonstrates why it is necessary to hold political elites and international institutions accountable. Pearson presents human rights concerns, based on Limburg Principles and Maastricht Guidelines, which provide a moral and international precedent for enforcing a transnational law upon states that refuse to adhere to the universal standards.[8]

## Recommendations for Future Study

The following are recommendations for future study.

1. Studies of the costs of nepotism and other activities associated with corruption.

2. Studies on how cultures successfully transition from tribal based government to a national government.

3. An examination of anti-corruption operations policies enhancing financial accountability in Afghanistan from 2009 to 2010.

The majority of the economic analyses in this study focused on how economic and government factors were influenced by corruption as measured by the CPI. The theoretical literature focused more on the act of bribery than on other activities also associated with corruption. Other activities associated with corruption need to be studied in order to obtain a more thorough and detailed assessment of the complete costs of corruption to the economic development of a country. These activities include, but are not limited to, the costs associated with nepotism, patronage, and misappropriation of government funds.

The cultural barriers that prevent the acceptance of a competitive market system, which prevent progress, are deemed as non-changeable. By studying historical examples of how countries transitioned from a tribal culture to a national one will help provide a framework and method for further cultural integration. These tactics could create change and affect nepotism within the Afghan culture.

Finally, a careful study of the activities enhancing accountability conducted by the U.S. military and civilian agencies involved with operations in Afghanistan in 2009 would potentially identify specific actions that improved the CPI by .1 from 2009 to 2010. Examples of these activities include the changes and policies of Contracting Command within the Department of Defense, the specific policies of Combined Joint Interagency Task Force-Shafafiyat, and the activities of other government and non-governmental organizations that provided developmental aid to Afghanistan. Afghanistan experienced a slight reduction in the corruption perception index in 2010 and several of the surveys conducted in Afghanistan in this period indicate a strong desire of Afghans to become less corrupt. A study of contracting practices and aid disbursement during this period could identify several effective methods with a direct, positive impact on corrupt practices for future application.

## Conclusion

According to Leff's theories, corruption provides a potential means for overcoming burdensome bureaucratic practices or breaching a government barrier that undermines economic development of the country.[9] Additional benefits of corruption include increasing social integration and initiating governmental and legal change.[10] However, very few cases exist where corruption directly benefited development or did not impose unacceptable economic costs. In order for corruption to be beneficial, it must be limited in scope and time and, most importantly, rapidly ended once the needed change in bureaucratic practices or leadership occurs. Over time, corruption expands and cripples a country, if it is allowed to persist.[11]

The conditions existing in Afghanistan demonstrate both the outcomes of a nation's acceptance of the risk of corruption and the validity of the empirical analyses of economic and political experts that disprove the theories of "beneficial corruption". In particular, the Afghan experience disproves the theory that corruption provides incentives that foster economic development.[12] Additionally, the studies that correlate government instability with violence further disprove the idea that corruption has economic benefit. The studies of Gyimah-Brempong and Voskanyan reflect these findings and specifically correlate increased corruption with irresponsible foreign aid.[13]

Corruption is crippling economic development in Afghanistan and reducing government legitimacy. The United States must promote reducing corruption as a key line of operation whenever it conducts operations to promote stable governments. The U.S. needs to emphasize the importance for global leaders to focus on anti-corruption practices. Globalization has increased the importance of economic responsibility and accountability because the effects of corruption extend beyond an individual country. In order to have real gains in the fight against corruption, efforts must focus beyond regional and state boundaries. These anti-corruption efforts would be enhanced by the establishment of a transnational organization or international body to develop a universal policy for government conduct and accountability. Its efforts would be enhanced by international endorsement of its ability to enforce adherence of governments to these guidelines. The author acknowledges the political challenges and sovereign rights that must be overcome, but effectively addressing corrupt practices of individual states will directly benefit the economic and political stability of the broader international community

---

[1]Belasco, 3.

[2]U.S. Government Accountability Office, "A*fghanistan: Key Issues for Congressional Oversight*, 4.

[3]Gyimah-Brempong, 207; Voskanyan, 26.

[4]Afghan Journalism Center; World Public Opinion.Org; Brigadier General H. R. McMaster.

[5]Chaikin, 97-99.

[6]Klitgaard, 77-82, 98-115, 134-155.

[7]Chaikin, 102.

[8]Pearson, 49.

[9]Leff, 313.

[10]Leff, 307-320.

[11]Werner, 199.

[12]Rose-Ackerman, 364-365.

[13]Gyimah-Brempong, 207; Voskanyan, 26.

# GLOSSARY

Corruption Perceptions Index. Transparency International's tool for measuring perceived corruption levels in a country. First launched in 1995, it has been widely credited with putting the issue of corruption on the international policy agenda. The CPI ranks almost 200 countries by their perceived levels of corruption, as determined by expert assessments and opinion surveys.

Gross Domestic Product. This measured value refers to the market value of all final goods and services produced within a country in a given period.

# APPENDIX A

## CONSENT AND USE AGREEMENT FOR ORAL HISTORY MATERIALS

You have the right to choose whether or not you will participate in this oral history interview, and once you begin you may cease participating at any time without penalty. The anticipated risk to you in participating is negligible and no direct personal benefit has been offered for your participation. If you have questions about this research study, please contact the student at:_bryan.b.coleman@us.army.mil; 580-574-0367_ or Dr. Robert F. Baumann, Director of Graduate Degree Programs, at (913) 684-2742.

To: Director, Graduate Degree Programs
Room 4508, Lewis & Clark Center
U.S. Army Command and General Staff College

1. I, _____, participated in an oral history interview conducted by

_____, a graduate student in the Master of Military Art and Science

Degree Program, on the following date [s]: _____ concerning

the following topic: _____.

2. I understand that the recording [s] and any transcript resulting from this oral history will belong to the U.S. Government to be used in any manner deemed in the best interests of the Command and General Staff College or the U.S. Army, in accordance with guidelines posted by the Director, Graduate Degree Programs and the Center for Military History. I also understand that subject to security classification restrictions I will be provided with a copy of the recording for my professional records. In addition, prior to the publication of any complete edited transcript of this oral history, I will be afforded an opportunity to verify its accuracy.

3. I hereby expressly and voluntarily relinquish all rights and interests in the recording [s] with the following caveat:

_____ None    _____ Other: _____

_____

I understand that my participation in this oral history interview is voluntary and I may stop participating at any time without explanation or penalty. I understand that the tapes and transcripts resulting from this oral history may be subject to the Freedom of Information Act, and therefore, may be releasable to the public contrary to my wishes. I further understand that, within the limits of the law, the U.S. Army will attempt to honor the restrictions I have requested to be placed on these materials.

_____
Name of Interviewee          Signature                          Date

_____
Accepted on Behalf of the Army by                                Date

# BIBLIOGRAPHY

## Books

Chaikin, David A. "Controlling Corruption by Heads of Government and Political Elites." In *Corruption and Anticorruption*, edited by Peter Larmour and Nick Wolanin, 97-118. Canberra, ACT, Asia Pacific Press, 2001.

Coleman, J. S. "Foundations on Social Theory." In *The Economics of Organized Crime*, edited by Gianluca Fiorentini and Sam Peltzman, 166. Cambridge, UK: Cambridge University Press, 1995.

Friedrich, Carl J. "Corruption Concepts in Historical Perspective." In *Political Corruption: Concepts and Contexts*, edited by Arnold Heidenheimer and Michael Johnson, 15-23. New Brunswick, NJ: Transaction Publishers, 2002.

Gardiner, J. "Defining Corruption." In *Political Corruption: Concepts and Contexts*, edited by Arnold Heidenheimer and Michael Johnson, 25-40. New Brunswick, NJ: Transaction Publishers, 2002.

Heidenheimer, Arnold. "Perspectives on the Perception of Corruption." In *Political Corruption: Concepts and Contexts*, edited by Arnold Heidenheimer and Michael Johnson, 141-154. New Brunswick, NJ: Transaction Publishers, 2002.

Heidenheimer, Arnold, and Michael Johnson. *Political Corruption: Concepts and Contexts*. New Brunswick, NJ: Transaction Publishers, 2002.

Holmes, Leslie. *The End of Communist Power*. New York: Oxford University Press 1993.

Huntington, Samuel P. "Modernization and Corruption." In *Political Corruption: Concepts and Contexts*, edited by Arnold Heidenheimer and Michael Johnson, 253-263. New Brunswick, NJ: Transaction Publishers, 2002.

Klitgaard, Robert. *Controlling Corruption.* Berkeley, CA: University of California Press, 1988.

Leff, Nathaniel. "Economic Development through Bureaucratic Corruption." In *Political Corruption: Concepts and Contexts*, edited by Arnold Heidenheimer and Michael Johnson, 307-320. New Brunswick, NJ: Transaction Publishers, 2002.

Lundberg, Kristen. "The Accidental Statesman: General Petraeus and the City of Mosul, Iraq." In US Army Command and General Staff College, *L200 Developing Organizations and Leaders: Advance Sheets and Readings,* 68. Fort Leavenworth, KS. USACGSC, December 2010.

Parker, Geoffrey. *The Military Revolution: Military Innovation and the Rise of the West, 1500-1800*, 2nd ed. Cambridge, UK: Cambridge University Press, 1988.

Pearson, Zoe. "An International Human Rights Approach to Corruption." In *Corruption and Anticorruption*, edited by Peter Larmour and Nick Wolanin, 30-61. Canberra, ACT, Asia Pacific Press, 2001.

Rose-Ackerman, Susan. "When is Corruption Harmful." In *Political Corruption: Concepts and Contexts*, edited by Arnold Heidenheimer and Michael Johnson, 353-371. New Brunswick, NJ: Transaction Publishers, 2002.

Sward, Koenraad. "The Sale of Public Offices." In *Political Corruption: Concepts and Contexts*, edited by Arnold Heidenheimer and Michael Johnson, 95-106. New Brunswick, NJ: Transaction Publishers, 2002.

Tanzi, Vito. "Corruption: Arm's-length relationships and Markets." In *The Economics of Organized Crime*, edited by Gianluca Fiorentini and Sam Peltzman, 161-180. Cambridge, UK: Cambridge University Press, 1995.

Werner, Simcha B. "The Development of Political Corruption in Israel." In *Political Corruption: Concepts and Contexts*, edited by Arnold Heidenheimer and Michael Johnson, 199-220. New Brunswick, NJ: Transaction Publishers, 2002.

## Scholarly Journals, Thesis, and Working Papers

Alam, Shahid. "Anatomy of Corruption: An Approach to the Political Economy of Underdevelopment." *The American Journal of Economics and Sociology* 48, no.4 (October 1989): 441-456.

Benhabib, Jess, and Aldo Rustichini. "Social Conflict, Growth and Income Distribution." *Journal of Economic Growth* 1 (1996): 125-142.

Gyimah-Brempong, Kwabena. "Corruption, Economic Growth, and Income Inequality in Africa." *Economics of Governance* 3 (2002): 183-209.

Kaufman, Daniel. "Corruption: The Facts." *Foreign Policy* 107 (Summer 1997): 114-130.

Kutan, Ali, and Thomas Douglas. "Does Corruption Hurt Economic Development? Evidence from the Middle East, North African, and Latin American Countries," Working paper, 2006.

Mauro, Paolo. "Corruption and Growth." *The Quarterly Journal of Economics* 110, no. 3 (2006): 681-712.

Myint-U, Thant. "Corruption: Causes, Consequences and Cures." *Asia-Pacific Development Journal* 7, no. 2 (December 2000): 33-58.

Nye, J. S. "Corruption and Political Development: A Cost-Benefit Analysis." *The American Political Science Review* 61, no. 2 (1967): 417-427.

Pei, Minxin. "Asia's Political Lessons." *China Business Review* (September 1999). http://www.chinabusinessreview.com/public/9909/pei.htm (accessed 15 March 2011).

Saastamoinen, Jani. "Wealth Distribution and Economic Growth." Discussion Papers 41, University of Joensuu, Finland, October 2006. http://epublications.uef.fi/pub/urn_isbn_952-458-871-4/urn_isbn_952-458-871-4.pdf (accessed 29 November 2011).

Sandholtz, Wayne, and William Koetzle. "Accounting for Corruption: Economic Structure, Democracy, and Trade." *International Studies Quarterly* 44 (2000): 31-50.

Swaleheen, Mushfiq, and Dean Stansel. "Economic Freedom, Corruption, and Growth." *Cato Journal* 27, no. 3 (2007): 343-358.

Tornell, A., and A. Velasco. "Why Does Capital Flow from Poor to Rich Countries? Interest Groups and Dynamic Games in Poor Countries." *Journal of Political Economy* 100 (1992): 1208-1231.

Treisman, Daniel. "The Causes of Corruption: A Cross-National Study." *Journal of Public Economics* 76, no. 3 (June 2000): 399-457.

Voskanyan, Frunzik. "A Study of the Effects of Corruption on Economic and Political Development in Armenia." Masters Thesis, American University of Armenia, November 2000.

## Government Documents

Belasco, Amy. *The Cost of Iraq, Afghanistan, and Other Global Was on Terror Operation Since 9/11.* Washington, DC: Congressional Research Service 2010. http://www.au.af.mil/au/awc/awcgate/crs/rl33110.pdf (accessed 15 March 2011).

Center for Army Lessons Learned. CALL Newsletter, No 10-64, *Afghan Culture: Observations, Insights, and Lessons.* Fort Leavenworth, KS: Government Printing Office, September 2010.

McMaster, Brigadier General H. R. VTC Briefing to Training Centers of Influence. Fort Leavenworth, KS. November 2010.

U.S. Department of Defense. *Quadrennial Defense Review Report*. Washington, DC: Government Printing Office, February 2010.

U.S. Government Accountability Office. *Afghanistan: Key Issues for Congressional Oversight.* April 2009. http://www.gao.gov/new.items/d09473sp.pdf (accessed 14 November 2011).

———. *Contract Management: DOD Vulnerabilities to Contracting Fraud, Waste, and Abuse*, 7 July 2006. http://www.goa.gov/products/GAO-06-838R (accessed 21 September 2011).

———. "Progress Toward Security and Stability in Afghanistan." Report to Congress. November 2010. www.defense.gov/pubs/November_1230_Report_FINAL.pdf (accessed 18 May 2011).

United States Agency for International Development. Afghanistan. *Assessment of Corruption in Afghanistan.* Washington, DC: Government Printing Office, 2009. http://pdf.usaid.gov/pdf_docs/PNADO248.pdf (29 November 2011).


Articles

Afghan Journalism Center. "Obama's Visit and Afghanistan's Corruption." http://www.ajc.af/english/component/content/article/47-category-name/84-obamas-visit-and-afghanistans-corruption (accessed 15 March 2011).

Chanrasekaren, Rajiv. "Karzai Rift Prompts U.S. to Reevaluate Anti-Corruption Strategy in Afghanistan." *The Washington Post*, April 2004. http://www.washington post.com/wp-dyn/content/article/2010/09/12/AR2010091203883.html (accessed 15 March 2011).

Douquet, Gregory, and Michael O'Hanlon. "A Realistic Anticorruption Strategy for Afghanistan." *The National Interest,* 13 October 2010. http://nationalinterest.org/commentary/realistic-anticorruption-4219 (accessed 15 March 2011).

The Economist. "Rough Riding: The Country's Tricky Politics get ever Trickier." *The Economist* 400, no. 8740 (July 2011): 34.

World Public Opinion.Org. "Afghan Approval of the Karzai Government and Western Forces, Though Still Strong, Is Declining," 14 December 2006. http://www.world publicopinion.org/pipa/articles/brasiapacificra/290.php?nid=&id=&pnt=290&lb=bras (accessed 15 March 2011).

Internet Sources

Army Acquisition Command. http://www.acc.army.mil/about (accessed 21 September 2011).

Candidate 40801? "What is the Impact of Corruption on Economic Development in the Newly Industrialized Countries of South East Asia?" *Political Corruption*, L2046, benaston.com/.../What%20is%20the%20impact%20of%20Corruption%20 o... United Kingdom (URL incomplete: found in Googledocs accessed 15 March 2011).

Center for Strategic International Studies. "Losing the War by Failing to Resource It and Manage the Resources That Were Provided." 2011. http://csis.org/files/ publication/110617_AfghanMetrics.pdf (accessed 21 July 2011).

Federal Election Commission. "The FEC and the Federal Campaign Finance Law." February 2010. http://www.fec.gov/pages/brochures/fecfeca.shtml# Contribution_Limits (accessed 17 September 2011).

Integrity Watch Afghanistan. "Afghan Perceptions and Experiences of Corruption." *National Survey 2010*. http://www.iwaweb.org/corruptionSurvey2010/ NationalCorruption2010.html (accessed 15 March 2011).

Livingston, Ian S., Heather Messera, and Michael O'Hanlan. "Afghanistan Index: Tracking Variable of Reconstruction & Security in Post-9/11 Afghanistan." http://www.brookings.edu/afghanistanindex (accessed 15 March 2011).

Special Inspector General to Afghanistan Reconstruction. 10th Quarterly Report, 30 January 2011. http://www.sigar.mil/pdf/quarterlyreports/Jan2011/Lowres/ Jan2011.pdf (accessed 21 September 2011).

Transparency International. "Corruption Perceptions Index, 2010." http://www. transparency.org/policy_research/surveys_indices/cpi/2010/results (accessed 15 March 2011).

Tzong-Shian Yu, and Dianqing Xu, eds. "From Crisis to Recovery: East Asia Rising Again?" in "What is the Impact of Corruption on Economic Development in the Newly Industrialized Countries of South East Asia?" Political Corruption, L2046, Candidate 40801, benaston.com/.../What%20is%20the%20impact%20of%20 Corruption%20o... United Kingdom (URL incomplete: found on Googledocs accessed March 2011).

U.S. Central Intelligence Agency. World Fact Book. "Country Comparison: GDP." https://www.cia.gov/library/publications/the-world-factbook/rankorder/ 2001rank.html. (accessed 15 March 2011).

———. World Fact Book. "Southwest Asia: Afghanistan." https://www.cia.gov/
library/publications/the-world-factbook/geos/af.html (accessed 15 March 2011).

United Nations Office on Drugs and Crime. *Corruption in Afghanistan*. 2010.
http://www.unodc.org/documents/data-and-analysis/Afghanistan/Afghanistan-
corruption-survey2010-Eng.pdf (accessed 21 July 2011).

World Bank. http://search.worldbank.org/data?qterm=afghanistan%20GDP%20
growth&language=EN (accessed 15 August 2011).

World Food Programme. Population and Demography. http://foodsecurityatlas.org/afg/
country/socioeconomic-profile/introduction (accessed 1 October 2011).

Oral History Interviews

Bulger, Major Ryan. Interviewed by author. Fort Leavenworth, Kansas, 18 May 2011.

Coolman, Major Joseph. Interviewed by author. Fort Leavenworth, Kansas, 6 July 2011.

Subject 1. Interviewed by author. Fort Leavenworth, Kansas, 12 July 2011.

www.ingramcontent.com/pod-product-compliance
Lightning Source LLC
Chambersburg PA
CBHW080312290526
45790CB00005B/2007